Before Their Time

Adult Children's Experiences
of Parental Suicide

EDITED BY

Mary Stimming
and
Maureen Stimming

TEMPLE UNIVERSITY PRESS
Philadelphia

Temple University Press, Philadelphia 19122
Copyright © 1999 by Temple University
All rights reserved
Published 1999
Printed in the United States of America

Text design by Gary Gore

⊖ The paper used in this publication meets the requirements of the
American National Standard for Information Sciences—Permanence of Paper
for Printed Library Materials, ANSI Z39.48-1984

Library of Congress Cataloging-in-Publication Data

Before their time : adult children's experiences of parental suicide /
edited by Mary Stimming and Maureen Stimming.
    p.   cm.
Includes bibliographical references and index.
ISBN 1-56639-654-9 (alk. paper). — ISBN 1-56639-655-7 (pbk. :
alk. paper)
    1. Aged—Suicide.   2. Parents—Death—Psychological aspect.
3. Adult children—Psychology.   4. Suicide victims—Family
relationship.   I. Stimming, Mary T. (Mary Theresa)
II.   Stimming, Maureen.
HV6545.2.B44   1999
155.9′37—dc21   98-8173

For our brothers and sisters in grief
who buried a parent before their time.
And most especially in memory of our parents
who died before their time.

It takes time to heal. It has been three years for me. I'm still healing. I never thought I'd love my mother the way I love her now. Her absence is not the burden it once was when she first took her life. In her forever-goneness I am learning to reweave my life with threads I've held on to from her life.

JoDe Rimar

One year and three weeks have passed since I received the news of my father's suicide. I am beginning to remember the law of gravity and to notice the friends still standing around me, reaching out in comfort and support. My husband steadfastly reminds me he loves me. We plan a picnic at the coast. I walk the dog in bare light, and I am grateful for the sun. I sing blessings to the rain that comes. I scroll through the happy memories of my father on his best afternoons. I meditate and exercise, rolling around in the green grass of the new sports park. I let the worries of money and worldly success roll by. And I keep writing. In remembering the joyful gifts of my life, I am coming home to myself for good.

Kathryn H. Gessner

Contents

Foreword

For the past eighteen years, I have worked closely with families wrenched by the death of a loved one by suicide. It was in this capacity that I came to know Mary and Maureen Stimming. Since 1979, LOSS (Loving Outreach to Survivors of Suicide) has provided a variety of programs designed to meet the special needs of survivors of suicide. Although I have been spared the tragedy of losing a family member through suicide, I have acquired some insights into the distinctive grieving patterns of those bereaved by suicide through my participation in LOSS.

I find it helpful to distinguish two aspects of grieving: Grief Work and the Grieving Process. Grief Work is the intense labor that goes on at the beginning of the grieving process. The Grief Work entails getting used to the grieving process. The Grief Work is very hard work. It taxes someone physically, emotionally, psychologically, and spiritually. Those working at their grief get tired quickly; they have trouble concentrating; they cry a lot and maybe get angry; they struggle to get through the day. During the intense Grief Work, feelings such as guilt and remorse are common among survivors of suicide. Often these reactions are irrational and exaggerated.

How long does Grief Work last? It is impossible to put a time limit on it, but it usually lasts one to two years. Grief Work begins abruptly—when the news of the suicide is received. The end of Grief Work is less noticeable. It is a gradual entry into the Grieving Process.

The Grieving Process never ends. We grieve throughout our lives for those significant people who have left us. The Grieving Process is living with the pain that loss causes. The pain ebbs and flows. Subsequent losses have special power to stir up previous losses in our lives. It is helpful for survivors to realize that they do not "get over it." They do, however, learn to live with it. That is the goal of any person in grief, not to get over the loss, but to learn to live with the resulting pain and the void in one's life. During the first several months following a suicide, survivors often ask me, "Will I ever laugh again? Will I ever enjoy life? Will the zest to live ever return?" My response to all these questions is "Yes." If one is willing to spend the time, the effort, and the tears, I can assure you that there is life after suicide. Life is forever changed, forever different; but there is joy.

In a manner distinctive of grief following suicide, survivors wrestle with the question, "Why?" There are a lot of theories about why people complete suicide. Research indicates that the vast majority of people who complete suicide are experiencing some type of mental or psychological disorder. In my opinion, the one thing that can safely be said about someone who completes suicide is that he or she believed, "I can no longer handle the pain in my life." In many instances the person has fought long and hard and has run out of steam. They are tired. They want rest—eternal rest.

I am convinced that suicide has nothing to do with the love and attention and commitment that family members and other key people in this person's life have offered. Knowing survivors as I do, I know much effort and devotion went into taking care of their loved one. Yet, survivors are often embarrassed or ashamed of how their loved one died. They do not want people to think less of their loved one because of the suicide. My position is that while suicide can be labeled a bad way to handle pain, the deceased person is not bad, nor is the family.

Survivors feel isolated from the world around them. Most people do not understand what it means to lose someone to suicide. Thus, it is most helpful for survivors of suicide to interact with each other and support each other and learn from each other. This can be done in many ways. It is my hope that this volume can be one of the sources of support and companionship that survivors so sorely need.

Rev. Charles T. Rubey, LCSW
Founder and Director, LOSS
Chicago, Illinois

Preface

Not a day goes by that I don't think of my father with, depending on my particular state of mind, happiness or sadness. Others do not realize that this way of losing a loved one is so different from death in the "usual" ways. The unanswered questions remain like a scab that won't heal. After my father committed suicide two years ago, I searched desperately for material to assist me in dealing with it. As an older adult taking his life, he is one of many, but little is written on the subject to help grown children deal with the loss and grief.

Mary Ann Schmidt

Our mother is one of the many older adults to whom Mary Ann Schmidt refers. Our mother was an intensely private person; hence it is with some trepidation that we share our experience. Because it is our experience we share, however, not hers, and because we have benefited from others' disclosures, we offer this book to fellow survivors, those close to them, and the clinicians who counsel them. All are looking for ways to "deal with the loss and the grief." It is our hope and firm intention that *Before Their Time* will serve as an aid in this arduous endeavor.

Adult children survivors of parental suicide are, sadly, an increasing population. Although it comes as a surprise to many, the age group most likely to complete suicide is the elderly. Tragically, suicide is a leading cause of death among adolescents. Individuals in this age bracket, however, die of relatively few causes. Causes of death among the elderly are more numerous; thus suicide does not rank as a leading cause of death. Nevertheless, in terms of the actual number of suicides, more persons over fifty than under thirty-five take their own lives. Given this grim demographic picture, it is plausible to assume that many, if not most, individuals over fifty years old who die by their own hand leave surviving children and that many of these children are eighteen or older at the time of their parent's death.

Yet, there is little to no lay or professional attention devoted to the experience of the adult children survivors of parental suicide. Overwhelmingly, discussions of the loss of a parent by suicide treat issues related to young children (e.g., how to inform them, grieving patterns among children). Adult children survivors (defined as those age eighteen or above at the time of a parent's death) are usually not mentioned in this context. However, these survivors, we believe, face not only the common difficulties associated with losing a loved one by suicide, but others that are specific to their status as both adult and child (including those found among younger children, e.g., identification with parent). This conviction was the catalyst for *Before Their Time*.

This work is intended primarily as a source of comfort for adult children survivors, their families, friends, and mental health professionals. The isolation that survivors of suicide often endure (as a result of social stigma, personal withdrawal, etc.) can be broached through the touch of other people's stories. The essays in this volume are meant to serve as companions on the journey of grief, which was so terribly and suddenly begun. This collection offers personal tales of pain and coping—assuring others that the agony they feel in a multitude of forms is not unique and can be endured. Second, this book aims at promoting the open discussion of suicide and its possible precursors, especially mental illness, and at sensitizing those who have not experienced such a loss to the distinctive aspects of grief following a suicide. Removing the social stigma that surrounds this subject comes only through extensive education. Although it is not an explicit feature of *Before Their Time*, this book has a pedagogical function—to enlighten others about suicide and its aftermath. Survivors of suicide often complain about the unthoughtful, even harsh, comments and treatment they receive from others. This work is a step toward eliminating this preventable compounding of grief.

Related to the above goals is a propaedeutic one. Researchers suspect a higher risk of suicide among those who have lost a family member by suicide, although studies confirming this are lacking. We hope that by exposure to the grief and resolution of other adult children survivors, readers who may be at risk will be encouraged to persevere. The resources listed in the fourth section are also intended as an interventionary measure for survivors. Ancillary to this objective is the goal of encouraging research into this population of suicide survivors. As noted above, the grief of adult children following parental suicide is rarely addressed in the professional literature. *Before Their Time* does not itself belong to the field of research. We make no efforts to interpret or analyze the stories we have collected. Nor did we dictate the content or style of the essays we received. We hope that this collection of first-person accounts will stimulate academic and clinical interest in this area such that further study will yield improved professional response to this group of survivors.

It has been thirty-six years since my mother killed herself. It seemed to me that I was finally ready to share how I felt about the event itself, that is, until I started writing. My daughter read my first draft and pointed out that it was like a news report. I gave the who, what,

> when—interestingly, I left out the how and where. I provided all
> the facts and no feelings.
>
> *Toni Rey*

This project evolved over several years. The emotional toll of chronicling such a personal and painful event caused us to postpone our plans repeatedly. In 1996, nearly six years after our mother's death, we submitted a proposal to several publishing houses. After securing a publishing commitment from Temple University Press, we sent a manuscript solicitation request to suicide survivor support groups throughout the United States. We asked the directors of these bereavement groups to distribute our information to appropriate persons. We sought to collect essays from a diverse demographic population. We also sought a spectrum of elapsed time between parental suicide and survivor reflection. We extended the option to contributors to remain anonymous. Although we feared that this would reinforce the stigma surrounding suicide, we were committed to preserving the privacy of those who requested it. Interestingly, only two of our authors exercised this option.

Our initial solicitation effort yielded numerous submissions from women, but none from men. Further efforts to obtain contributions from male survivors included networking through the American Association of Suicidology, the Illinois Association of Social Workers, personal contacts, and the Internet. The challenge of identifying male survivors willing to share their stories echoes the difficulty that researchers encounter obtaining male participants for clinical studies of suicide survivors. Like the researchers, we found that women were more emotive and more inclined to write. A few of the male authors represented in *Before Their Time* chose to be interviewed rather than to pen a narrative of their experience. These men retained final approval over the chapters that appear above their names.

The demographics of American suicide are reflected in the submissions we received. In the United States, most persons who die by suicide are white, middle-class males. The category that elicited the largest number of essays was "Loss of a Father," and all contributors are Caucasian. (Accounts of the experiences of minorities and diverse ethnic groups are needed. "The Aftermath of Suicide among African-Americans" by Donna Holland Barnes is one effort to redress the underreported status of this survivor population [Ph.D. dissertation, Northeastern University, 1997].) Most completed suicides are by persons with a past or current psychiatric disorder (e.g., major depression, bipolar disorder, substance abuse), and these diagnoses are noted in the majority of essays. One effect of parental mental illness is the reversal of the usual parent-child relationship. Many adult children survivors express feelings of guilt similar to those of parents who have lost a child by suicide. Despite obvious differences, parents and children share similar responsibilities — especially when the child is an adult empowered to participate in his or her parent's care. To our surprise, we received no essays describing the aftermath of a suicide precipitated by severe or terminal physical illness. The ongoing public discussion of physician-assisted suicides suggests that a number of adult children either have participated in their parent's suicide or have had prior knowledge of it. The particular grief of these survivors remains unexplored in this volume.

This book is arranged in four main sections. The first and second sections deal with the experiences of daughters and sons in response to the suicides of mothers and fathers respectively. Between the essay sections are brief reflections (Intermezzos) on particular themes (e.g., suicidal feelings, issues concerning grandchildren of the deceased). The third section contains essays by ourselves and our two brothers — four perspectives on a common loss. The fourth section functions as a resource guide. It features chapters from two of the leading national experts on suicide and survivors of suicide. David C. Clark, director of the Center for Suicide Research and

Prevention at Rush-Presbyterian–St. Luke's Medical Center in Chicago, analyzes suicide in later life. John L. McIntosh, professor of psychology at Indiana University in South Bend and past president and a member of the board of directors of the American Association of Suicidology, provides a review of the research literature on survivors of suicide. Following Professor McIntosh's chapter are a brief annotated bibliography of key texts in the suicide survivor literature and an abridged national directory of suicide survivor support groups.

Almost without exception, the first drafts we received contained lengthy and detailed descriptions of the parent's suicide. The compulsion of suicide survivors to speak of the horror of their loved one's death is not unusual. Repeating the details often helps survivors accept the reality of their loss and allows them to remember it in a more meaningful context. Nor is it surprising that our authors felt free to share with us the most graphic details of their loss. Suicide continues to carry a heavy social stigma, and survivors often fear that others will greet their experience with revulsion and accusation. Hence, when survivors find an accepting and sympathetic audience, they often launch into an explicit description of the trauma.

These factors account, in large part, for the character of the drafts we received. But other dynamics were apparent as well. Many of the authors commented in their cover letters that they had never before related the events of their parent's death. Most of the men had sought no counseling or support group. Outside of their immediate families, we were the first to hear their stories. Most of the women do participate in a local survivor support group but, they report, their stories are often marginalized in favor of those of parental survivors of adolescent suicide. Nearly all authors indicated that they had met few, if any, other adult children survivors of parental suicide. Thus, it is our opinion that being an adult child compounds the need, typical of all survivors, to repeat the tale of loss. Adult children survivors are unlikely to know persons among the general survivor population who share their particular type of loss, and they are likely to encounter minimal interest. If we were to make one recommendation based on the essays we received, it would be addressed to leaders of suicide survivor groups: Be alert to your group's tendency to enshrine one relationship (usually the parent-child) as the apex of loss and the consequent propensity to minimize others (e.g., child-parent, sibling).

The challenge facing us as editors and fellow survivors was how to handle the excruciatingly raw details. Although we remain sensitive to the survivors' desire to share them, we chose to limit or exclude graphic accounts of how the deceased took his or her life and of the physical devastation caused by the means of death. This difficult decision rests on two bases: One, we want to respect the privacy of the deceased and that of other members of the surviving family; two, the focus of *Before Their Time* is not the suicide per se, but its effects and the process of surviving.

Several themes recur across the essays' descriptions of the adult child survivor's experience. Chief among these is anxiety about the possibility of future suicides—by one's self, one's siblings, one's children. Survivors confided fears that their parent's actions were somehow "inheritable." To some extent, this concern grows out of a sober assessment of genetic predisposition to certain forms of mental illness and of influential psychological patterns. Some fear stems from the recognition that a completed suicide in the family breaks a profound taboo. Suicide is a concrete option in a way it was not before the parent's death. But some aspects of the fear of one's own eventual suicide hinge on a mystical sense of destiny: Aren't we instructed from our earliest days to emulate our parents?

Many authors, especially the women who lost a mother, comment on their feelings of abandonment. A parent's love for his or her child is a standard measure of unconditional love. Countless tales abound of the heroic, often self-sacrificing, actions of parents on behalf of their children. From the dramatic (entering a burn-

ing house to save a child) to the noble but pedestrian (shoulder-
ing grueling work for the sake of a child's welfare), parental love is
extolled as the definition of selfless love. Parents often display su-
perhuman endurance in meeting their children's needs. In light
of these realities, how ought one to think about the parent-child
bond when the giver and sustainer of life ends his or her existence?
The essays poignantly describe the pain that adult survivors wrestle with on this score — a pain not lessened by their mature cognitive abilities.

Feelings of abandonment and the desire to recount the details
of the death are common among all survivors of suicide. Other
themes on which the contributors comment belong more uniquely
to the adult children's experience. For example, many authors write
of the burden of new responsibilities, especially financial, and of
conflicting role demands. Young children who lose a parent to suicide may find themselves expected to grow up faster and to take on
the role of surrogate parent to other siblings or some of the roles of
a spouse to a surviving parent. These young children do not have to
deal with family finances, however, and their roles typically are not
as numerous or as demanding as those of adult children survivors.
Adult children, who often have their own spouses, children, and careers, find their performance in these multiple roles challenged and
reshaped by their grief experience. The essays suggest the extent to
which their grief interacts with the exigencies and complexities of
adult life.

Although the authors do not represent a statistically significant
sample, some differences in themes between the men's and
women's essays do appear. The men admit to a certain reluctance
to face the full reality of their loss, and as suggested above, they are,
as a group, less likely to have participated in a suicide survivor support group. Most men indicate that their parent's suicide did not sig-
nificantly alter their personal or professional status. In contrast, the
women recount the tremendous stress placed on their marriages by

their grief. Almost all the female contributors who divorced since their parents' deaths name the strain of the grief as contributing to the end of their marriages. Women too write more frequently of the impact of the suicide on their professional choices. Several report major and minor changes in the direction of their careers—changes directly attributed to the manner, and not merely the fact, of their parent's death.

One of the original submissions, later withdrawn by its author, explored the dynamics of the adult child's response to parental suicide following childhood sexual molestation. This courageous woman gave voice to a particularly stigmatized group. Surely other adult children survivors of parental suicide share her tragic history and wrestle with the complex emotions that follow their abuser's death. We respect the author's decision not to publish her story, but we make note of it here for the sake of those who find themselves in the unusually lonely position she so eloquently described. The broader issue she forces to center stage is one with which many survivors and support groups are most uncomfortable—reactions to the suicide of a destructive, even violent, individual.

To every survivor who contacted us and most especially to every contributor, we owe a tremendous debt of gratitude. Their interest in this project confirmed our decision to proceed. Their desire to provide for fellow adult children survivors the resource they wish they had available at their hour of greatest need made this project possible. Their honest and moving reflections on their experiences, and their cheerful willingness to revise, have more than fulfilled our highest expectations for this collection. Their insightful narratives affirm our conviction that there are distinctive features of adult children's grief following parental suicide. It is our collective hope that *Before Their Time* will bring comfort to survivors and increased understanding to those who live and work with them.

Mary Stimming
Maureen Stimming

Acknowledgments

Before Their Time is not a pioneer in exploring the multifaceted phenomenon of suicide survivor grief. We are grateful for the works of courageous pathbreakers such as Iris and Jim Bolton, Betsy Ross, Victoria Alexander, Karen Dunne-Maxim, Ed Dunne, Lois and Sam Bloom, and Christopher Lukas. They are but several of the survivors of suicide who by defying public stigma and sharing their private pain encourage others toward full lives after suicide loss. We must also acknowledge the work of researchers and clinicians, most notably John McIntosh, who have dedicated their professional lives to assisting survivors and to preventing the tragedies that add to our ranks.

Many individuals and groups contributed directly or indirectly to this work. Our original idea would not have developed save for the assistance of Jack Connor, Jim Langford, and our ever-patient and ever-encouraging editor, Michael Ames. The process of collecting and editing essays would have permanently stalled except for the help of the American Association of Suicidology, Mary Lou DeMaria-Berhang, Karen Dunne-Maxim, and Tim Grzeczka. We would not have seen the possibility of comforting others had we not benefited from the restoring strength of others: from members of the LOSS program who are a constant source of inspiration; from recently retired LOSS director Therese Gump, a model of the reassurance that "joy will return to your lives"; and from LOSS founder Rev. Charles Rubey, who is a rock amid the storm. We have been fortunate to know other healers of our broken hearts and spirits: professionals and compassionate friends and family who are treasured beyond all telling. Our father Charles Stimming and his wife Margaret have supported this work since its inception—a sanction from which many parents would shrink. Mary's husband Louis Centorcelli has been, as always, computer guru, deciding vote, and anchor. He has earned the highest honor we can imagine—full membership among the Stimming siblings. Finally, our deepest thanks to all the contributors. Through their generosity, they forge a legacy of suicide more powerful than sorrow and agony; they give hope.

M.S.
M.S.

I

Loss of a Mother

A Joyful Spirit

Her name was Joy and that's what she was. Once she stepped into your life you never forgot her. She was respected and loved by everyone who met her. Throughout her life she had endured heartache and tragedy. She lost her father, sister, and two brothers in the prime of their lives. Her nineteen-year marriage ended in divorce. She suffered periodically from depression. Through all her hardship and struggles, she pulled herself up. Her determination to survive was tremendous, her spirit so strong. She was only fifty-seven when she died.

She raised five daughters. She was my light when I needed direction, my rock. I married young and found myself struggling to keep the marriage together while working and raising a family. Mom supported me—emotionally and in many practical ways. I named my first daughter after my mother, as I wanted a part of her grandma to be with her always. My mother was always a proud and active grandma. Thus, Mom's reaction when I had my third child was particularly strange. She didn't get a present for the new baby, she didn't call as often, she seemed preoccupied by trivial things. I was so wrapped up in the new baby that I didn't read much into these changes.

Then five weeks after the baby was born, Mom killed herself. At first, I was filled with anger. How could she have truly loved us? How could she leave her own grandchildren? Why couldn't she make it one more day? Wasn't our love enough to make her stay alive?

My three children (ages fourteen, six, and five weeks) kept me from falling apart. I had to be strong for them. They had depended on their grandma as much as I had. I never hid the truth from them. I never gave them the horrible details—but I never lied. Any questions that they had deserved an honest answer. Always, the hardest question to face was "Why, Mommy?" How could I respond when I too searched so hard for the answer? I told them that she was sad, so sad that the pain she felt was unbearable. My answer haunted me later, sometimes even today. If I was having an extremely hard day, my precious children would sometimes ask, "Mommy, are you sad? Are you sad like Grandma was?" I could see the fear in their eyes. I could only reassure them time and time again that I was okay, that sometimes people do feel sad but they are all right. Other times my children were so angry they would scream out at their grandma. Punches thrown at doors and walls would express the depth of the anger. One child had been particularly close to my mother. She was the buddy, the soul mate. Now she was gone. No one could fill her shoes. Shortly after her death, this child was so upset at Grandma's betrayal that the words, "I'm going to kill myself. Grandma did, so can I," came out. I was devastated. A caring counselor came to our rescue and helped the children sort out their complex emotional reactions.

Somehow we made it through the firsts: Christmas, birthdays, all those holidays that Mom made more special. I sheltered myself in my home. As long as my kids were around me and my sisters nearby, I felt safe. Nothing could happen to them if they were close by. In the beginning, it seemed I drowned in tears. But slowly, very slowly, the pain in my heart began to lessen. The baby brought joy to us all. She reaffirmed life. She was a new beginning. Going through the everyday routine of life became less of a struggle. Laughter became real again.

But while I fought to keep my children and myself going, my

marriage fell apart. Our marriage was fragile before my mom's death. It was not strong enough to survive the demands of grieving. Within two years, I had lost my mom and my marriage. It wasn't long after that that I almost lost myself.

After the divorce, I decided to go back to school. I had to earn a decent living. I had to start all over with my life. The anxiety of leaving the safety of my home and family overwhelmed me. After pulling myself up day after day, I just could not pull anymore. I was physically and emotionally exhausted. I would try to sleep, but I would wake up every hour, my heart racing madly. I tried to eat, but the food choked me. For the first time in my life, I had lost my will, my spirit. I wanted to crawl in a dark corner and be left alone. I started crying on a Thursday. The next day, I was still crying. My sister took me to a mental health clinic. I hadn't stopped crying. The nurse was wonderful. She knew I was having a breakdown severe enough to require hospitalization. I had no insurance, no money. She found a hospital that had a community bed for people in situations like mine. It allowed me to get the help I needed at no cost.

The doctor who was assigned to me came in that night. He pronounced me suicidal. He said I needed to face the fact that I was like my mother. I argued with him. I got mad at him. I was not like her. I WANTED TO LIVE. But slowly I realized that what he was trying to say to me had some truth to it. A propensity to depression is hereditary. My mother's father had taken his life. My mother fought all her life with depression. It finally won. But I was determined to break the cycle. I reached out for help. Mental illness is not a shameful thing. What's shameful is not getting help. I can now say I have a small idea of the hell your mind can put you through. I lived through a relatively short episode of what my mother experienced. But I reached out for help and found hope.

It's been a long journey back—but a worthwhile one that has enabled me to live my life to the fullest. After my recovery, I enrolled in a vocational-technical school and received a certificate in building maintenance. I was the first female to graduate with this degree. I now have a dream job with the National Park Service. I am learning to love again. I have met a wonderful man who holds me when the tears fall. He knows my grief and understands my life. My children are surviving right beside me. They lost their grandma, their dad, and their way of life. To say it has been easy would be a lie. To say we don't struggle at times with Mom's death, even today, would be an even greater lie. But now when we talk about Grandma, it is with fondness and smiles more than anger and tears.

I am in control of my life now. My children have seen and know the determination it takes to keep going. I hope I have given them the strength to persevere when all seems lost. Through all our struggles we have survived together. My spirit has survived along with me, and I see that spirit in my children. I believe this spirit belongs to my mother. It's the part of her that has been with us all along.

Treva Gordon

Treva Gordon was thirty-six in 1991 when her
mother, aged fifty-seven, completed suicide.

Home and Beyond

I heard the fear in my big sister's voice when she called me with the news of my mother's suicide. My world went black. I felt ice-cold. Through my fog, I notified my husband and began preparations for my family to travel the few hours to my sister's home. I remember pulling into her driveway. The warm September night had a gentle breeze. Her porch light was on, the front door was standing open. The minute the car turned into the driveway, she came to us with hugs and tears. From that moment on, I was back in the womb of my family of origin. Now there were just the two of us. Growing up, it had always been the four of us together, the four of us against the world. Without our parents, Barb and I were orphans, and suddenly it was just the two of us against the world. I was one month away from my thirty-second birthday, and it felt as if I were once again eight years old and my big sister was protecting me from snowball attacks.

If only I had realized then that I was excluding my own precious family—my husband and my four children. I look back now and believe that the distancing from my husband began that very night. It ended in our divorce six years later. I did not turn to him because I assumed he could not possibly understand what I was going through; his parents were still alive! Perhaps there were problems in the marriage before my mom's death, but there was nothing of great significance. We had celebrated our tenth anniversary days before Mom's death. We were happy and at peace. Then came this death, and I turned to my sister and retreated into my family of origin, leaving my own family behind. I wonder if my husband sensed my distance that first night. Barb suggested that I sleep in her room and that he bunk with my brother-in-law on the pull-out couch. He insisted that I was to stay with him but, in the end, it didn't matter since Barb and I sat at the dining room table talking most of the night.

After the funeral, my husband and children went home to Indiana, and I stayed behind for two weeks to complete the paperwork of death and to begin the process of cleaning out a nine-room house. I suspect that I also wanted to avoid returning to Indiana. Somewhere in the back of my mind I knew that this event presented a special burden to my husband. He was dealing with a relatively new job as well as with four children who ranged in age from eleven months to eight years old. I was grateful that he was parenting and caring for the children. I knew they were in good hands. We talked on the phone almost every night during those two weeks, but it seemed too hard to explain my pain to him. With my sister, however, I could talk and share so easily. Even when I finally returned to Indiana, I wasn't "there." I was sorting things I had brought back, and I was planning my next trip "home" to Mom's house.

Thanks to the suggestion of a friend, I began to see a grief therapist. Throughout this process, I returned to my hometown two days a week for the next year. I spent one day cleaning out the family home with Barb and the next day seeing the therapist. Although these two days were healing for me, they created a gulf between me and my husband and children. Did I see that then? Absolutely not. Every week I returned to Indiana with a car loaded with furniture and memories. Boxes and boxes of precious mementos came back to Indiana. Every week I hauled in things and sorted through them. I don't remember if the children helped or if I even explained what most of it was. I was either crying, angry, or simply numb. I tried to talk to my husband and tell him what it was like, and I know that he tried to listen and understand. But we weren't in this together. I was living two lives. Five days a week, I was a wife and mother. I cooked, cleaned, baked, drove carpools, and tried to block out the death of my mother. Then I got behind the wheel of my car and drove to my hometown, where for two days I became little sister again. I was cared for and nurtured by Barb's family—

a family who, unlike my own, saw their mom crying and out-of-sorts during the week. I went back to the house where I was raised, I was helped by the neighbor who had always been a second mother to me, and I was a child again in my parents' home.

What would I have done differently? Perhaps the entire family needed to come along on occasion and help with Mom's house. I needed to be with them and cry with them. I thought I was protecting the children, but I was hurting them as well by not including them. Once in a while I would bring one of the children to my hometown with me. I brought one child to see my grief therapist to make sure that she was okay. After he pronounced her healthy, I heaved a sigh of relief. I felt that I had done a good thing for her by taking her to a therapist and that I could rest assured that all was well. Another time I brought a different child to visit old friends. She had been telling me that if I "just would go to Grandma's house she would be there." When I tried to talk to her about Grandma's death, my words fell on deaf ears. It wasn't until she and I walked through the partially emptied house room by room that she was able to understand that Grandma didn't live there any more. It was at that moment that she was able to cry.

Now, many years later, the older ones tell me that it was hard being with their father so much. At times, he would be crabby and out-of-sorts, and they missed me. If only I had known that then, maybe it would have made a difference. I'm sure my husband didn't say how difficult it was because he thought that he was being supportive in his own way. He hadn't had any preparation for this either.

Those first holidays were a study in avoidance. We spent the first Thanksgiving at Barb's. I had enough champagne before dinner that I took a nap and awoke in time for dessert! Christmas was at our home in Indiana. Barb and her family arrived so late on Christmas Eve that my kids were in bed. The youngest awoke sick on Christmas morning. I didn't feel so well, either. All I remember of that day is watching the kids open gifts and thinking, "Who cares? Mom is dead. Why are we doing this?"

Seven months after Mom's death, I began the training class for a local Suicide Prevention Center. At one session, the director handed out brochures for the American Association of Suicidology (AAS) and a notice about a suicide conference that was being held in Iowa. I longed to go . . . a suicide conference, what could I learn? That October conference was so powerful that even as I write this I feel once again the strength that rose in me as I heard the word "survivor." The pieces of the puzzle were beginning to fall into place. I listened to Iris Bolton and Betsy Ross talk respectively of their son's and husband's deaths. I did not know that I was crying until the tears began to drop on my blouse. I was mesmerized! I was a survivor of suicide! I wasn't crazy! I was grieving!

I came home eager to start a survivors of suicide support group. I sent for Betsy Ross's literature about starting a Ray of Hope group, but I felt so overwhelmed by the paperwork that I put that idea aside. Later I did begin a group for suicide survivors. This group grew out of a conference I co-sponsored with my former counselor. At the conclusion of the one-and-a-half-day conference, an audience participant asked: "Where is a survivors of suicide group?" Since there wasn't a group, I told her that any interested survivor could come to the college library on Monday night, and we would begin a group. Seven people (including me) showed up, and fourteen years later we are still going strong with an average of twenty-five people at each monthly meeting and a mailing list for the newsletter in the hundreds.

Over the years, I have not met many other people who have lost a parent to suicide. Our monthly meetings consist mostly of parents and spouses of those who have died by suicide. At an AAS conference years ago I was able to talk with three other women who had lost mothers. I was hungry to talk with others who had lost moms. My own sister and I have grieved so differently. As a direct result of my mom's death, I started studying suicide. Today I run a support group and direct a Suicide Prevention Hot Line. My sister and I talk about Mom's death, but Barb mostly focuses on parental issues rather than the suicide. Yes, there were conflicts because of the way we grieved. She was angry at Mom and didn't want to talk about it. She came to the support group for the first time on the tenth anniversary of its founding, which meant a great deal to me. She remains on the mailing list for our newsletter and periodically makes donations.

What was it like to lose my last remaining parent? It made me feel that I was an adult. There was no parent to go to for advice. It seems that no matter how old one gets, our parents still have the answers. I see this relationship continue with my friends and their mothers. Who will remember me as a child? Who will love me like that again? The answer is a simple, "No one." My mother loved me completely and unconditionally. She was very proud of me as a person, as a daughter, as a mother to my own children. She could tell me things that I did as a child and compare them to things my own kids were doing by saying, "That's just what you did" or, "You used to have that same look on your face." I miss that. My sister is nearly nine years older, and she can tell many stories about me as a child, but my kids can't go to anyone to hear the stories that even Barb can't remember.

Mom and I were very close. We could tell each other anything and talk for hours about everything. We loved to go shopping together and out to lunch. I remember one bright, clear, crisp day when we were shopping. I was in my early twenties, she in her early fifties. I saw a mother and her daughter coming out of Fields as we were entering. The mother was in her seventies, the daughter in her later fifties. One had gray hair, the other's hair was snow white. The mother had her arm through her daughter's, and they were laughing and chatting much as my mother and I were that day. I can remember saying to my mom, "That will be us someday," to which she replied, "I won't live that long." I know I clucked about her comment and indicated she was being foolish. Now that phrase often comes back to me. Did she say that because her own mother died at thirty-six, or . . . was suicide an option even then?

What was it like to lose a parent to suicide? Horrible, terrifying, and something for which no one is ever prepared. Suicide is never completely forgotten or forgiven. When people who don't know me very well ask how my parents died, I know that the word suicide will be a shock. And then the usual questions follow, "Did you know she was sad?" "Was she depressed?" Through my mother's death, suicide became an option for me and for my family. While it was never even thought of before, now that the family matriarch ended her life, the option is there. I hate that. I worry for my children. They loved their grandma and looked up to her. We have talked at length about her pain and her need for help—someone to talk to, someone to help her cope. Suicide is a way of coping with pain, I tell them, but there are certainly healthier ones.

What were (and are) the difficult times that trigger the pain and loss anew? Family events, for one; especially times when the generations gather in celebration. For example, confirmations have been difficult. My oldest daughter was confirmed in the Lutheran faith five and one-half years after Mom's death. I remember the waves of grief crashing over me as I ached for her presence that day. Two years later I went through similar emotions at my elder son's confirmation. In a newsletter column, I wrote:

> My family of origin has been Lutheran on both sides—as far back as to when Martin Luther nailed the Ninety-five Theses on the church door. A tradition was continuing. I could almost feel the presence of my ancestors around me. For this young man, a rite of

passage was occurring. In the eyes of the church, he was an adult. I recalled his Baptism in the same church. Both sets of grandparents were present that day. Now, his maternal grandparents were dead and his paternal grandfather lay dying in a nursing home. As the tears fell, my ten-year-old and my eight-year-old children began the questions: "Why are you crying?" "What's the matter?" I shook my head, indicating I did not wish to speak (or could not). All of a sudden, the ten-year-old's face looked as if she'd made a startling discovery. She leaned over me and whispered to the eight-year-old, "It's about Grandma 'cause she died." Little Mr. Eight-year-old nodded with the wisdom only an eight-year-old can possess and said, "Oh, yeah, it's about Grandma." And I guess that really sums it up. It was about Grandma. There will never be a family gathering where she isn't remembered or thought about.

My mom could have been at her grandchildren's confirmations. Unfortunately, years earlier she made a decision that precluded her presence at these occasions. Her pain was such that to think ahead to this day would have been unthinkable. And . . . yet . . . she was there. Her love and her guidance were felt strongly that day. She was there in her grandchildren's smiles, and in the presence of her two daughters seated side by side.

Mom has been missed at high school graduations and other family events. I felt her absence at my own graduation. Two years after Mom's death, I entered a graduate program in counseling. I knew that I wanted to do for other people what my counselor had done for me. I wanted to help. I wanted to take my experience and help others. I know now that this is quite common. I had a wonderful advisor who got me to write about Mom's death. I had processed it and intellectualized it; he made me *feel* it. Only as we worked on that paper did I finally let go in front of people other than family and close friends.

There have been other wonderful changes in my life. I am a grandmother now too. The birth of my first grandchild was a bittersweet event as I thought of Mom and how very much she loved babies. She would have been only seventy-three-years young when her first great-grandchild was born. How she would have loved that! And in May of 1996, I remarried. For a while, it bothered me that Bill never knew my parents, but then, I really didn't know his either. I was always grateful that he was in the field of psychology because he had a clear understanding of my grief process and my related work. He has been and continues to be enormously understanding and supportive.

My wedding day was filled with joy and happiness. But . . . as always . . . in the back of my mind was my mom. I felt her presence that day as I walked down the aisle. I felt her approval, her excitement, and, above all, her love. The old wish kicked in as the minister began the service. I wished for her to be there. I could feel the tears stinging my eyes; then a peace came over me. I could almost hear her voice saying, "It's okay, Stephie, I'm here." She was there. She was in the form of my sister sitting in the front row beaming with pride and happiness. She was there in the gentle face of the minister. She was there in the faces of my children and in the faces of my niece and nephew. And she was there in Bill's eyes and in the gentleness of his voice as he said his vows. That warm May day was filled with flowers and sunshine and gentle breezes. She was there . . . she was in it all. . . . I didn't doubt, have never doubted, her love for me. I doubted her love for herself but never her love for me. Her last act did not in any way diminish her love for me, or mine for her.

Stephanie Weber

Stephanie Weber was thirty-one in 1979 when
her mother, aged sixty-one, completed suicide.

Center Piece

My mother had stayed with me that weekend. We had a yard sale at my apartment complex. She did not seem herself—she was upset that people were haggling over prices, she kept repeating things. When she left to go home, she hugged me and said goodbye. She did not wave as she drove away. She looked forward and headed home. Suddenly I felt unsettled. I had felt this way two weeks before, too. To calm my vague fears, I called Mom later that night. I continued to feel ill at ease, but I didn't want to overreact.

The next day, I received a call at work that there was a family emergency, I panicked. My mind raced. Was my husband in an accident? Was my father hurt? Had my mother done something to herself? Once my mind grasped that possibility, it would not let go of that idea. When I saw my husband, Troy, waiting for me, I knew by his face that something terrible had happened. His hard words confirmed it, "Your mother committed suicide this morning." I screamed and cried as Troy cradled me on the ground. I was furious. My mother had left me. That is the worst feeling in the world.

Every part of my life has been affected in some way by my mother's death. My relationships with my husband, my dad, and my sisters have all changed. I've realized that one person can make all the difference in the world. Without Mom at the center, none of our lives will ever be the same again. But as long as we remember her, she will always be a part of us.

Husband

The sudden loss of a mother can really test the relationship between a husband and wife. My husband has been there through it all: the crying, the hurting, the silence, and the anger. He is still here now as I cope and look back at the many memories I have about my mother. But he gets frustrated that he cannot make the pain go away. Troy tries in every way to help, but at times I just want to be alone. I withdraw to a place where no one else can be. He tries to understand, but the feelings that I have are my own. Sometimes even I do not understand why I feel the way I do. The best thing that he has done for me is to listen when I am upset, not try to "fix" it. No matter how hard he tries, he will never be able to fix this.

The first year after my mother's death was especially stressful for us. I was so depressed. I can hardly remember anything that we did together. I just remember feeling the hurt and not wanting to do anything at all. He tried so hard to cheer me up. But I did not want any help; I wanted to cry and let the hurt come out. I kept to myself; we really did not have a relationship that year. It has now been three years, and we have been able to concentrate on "us" again. We were talking one day, and it just hit us that the terrible thing in our life was not in the middle of our relationship anymore. Even though there have been some very difficult times, I feel that we have grown closer through them.

Father

It hurt so much to see my dad wounded by my mother's suicide. Dad found her that terrible morning. He had spent twenty-eight years with my mother, now he did not know what was to come. Everything had been laid out and planned, and now there were only question marks and much loneliness. Within days after my mother's death, he asked my sisters and me if it would be all right if he got married again. We kind of laughed about it and jokingly gave him the guidelines for his new wife. I really did want him to have someone to do things with and share his life. I just was not ready to deal with it now or anytime soon. My mother was not physically here, but her spirit surrounded me. I needed to deal with the pain of missing her first before I could let anyone else be in the place where she should still be.

It seemed that we were closer than ever right after Mom died. During the first year following her death, my family continued to get together and do those types of activities we had always enjoyed as a family. But over time, it seemed that my father increasingly wanted to do things on his own. That is when he started dating. I was torn: I wanted my dad to be happy, but I still wanted my original family. When my dad started dating one special woman, our family time became nonexistent. When I came home to visit, I was unable to spend any time alone with my dad. Nor did we do anything together as a family. He just wanted to be with her and only her. My dad often left my youngest sister, a teenager, alone. This really upset me, I knew that she needed someone there for her after all that had happened. I was angry with my dad because he was not there for her. He was not there for any of us.

Eight months later, my father married this woman. I wanted to cry through the entire ceremony. I just kept thinking about my mother. I felt that our family did not mean anything to my dad anymore. I suspect that he does not want to think about our "original" family because it hurts too much. Instead, he talks about his new stepdaughter and stepson. It is his new family. I feel like an outsider looking in. There have been so many ups and downs with my dad and his new wife. We all started off on the wrong foot. We never had enough time to get to know one another. Our family and our traditions are gone.

I do not feel that my dad has been there for me or tried to understand my feelings or my pain. When I have stated how I feel, I have been told that I am unwelcome to come home. My dad's wife has been upset because I did not send her a Mother's Day card. She never said anything to me about it; I was just told I was not welcome to come home. I was so hurt by my mother's death, and now I have to deal with all of this. I guess that things have been better lately. I have really been trying, but I am so afraid of what I may inadvertently do that will cause an uproar or turn my dad against me. I do not understand my dad. I don't know what has caused these changes in our relationship: Is he so full of pain or has he changed so much that I do not know him anymore?

Sisters

My middle sister turned seventeen the day after our mother committed suicide. My other sister was only thirteen years old when Mom died. With both sisters, I felt that they wanted me to do the things that Mom would have done. I tried to take on the role as best I could. But I was not Mom, and I could not do her job. A sister just isn't your mother. Growing up, we sisters were not particularly close. But through this tragedy, our relationships have deepened.

The effects of my mother's death have been felt in all the most central relationships in my life—in some cases, her death has so-lidified and strengthened; in others, it has weakened and warped. My hope is that her memory will help bring healing to them all.

Kimberley Garnhart

Kimberley Garnhart was twenty-four in 1993 when her mother, aged forty-nine, completed suicide.

Changes of Direction

I miss my mother's beauty. As a child I used to enjoy just watching her. I would watch her move about the kitchen as she cooked; I felt warm and nurtured. It is the mere presence of my mother that I miss. Recently, I saw a clerk in a department store who resembled my mother. I found myself following her around. My mother loved to go shopping; seeing this clerk in the same surrounding triggered a great feeling of loss. I just wanted to go up and hug this woman. I felt angry also. I wanted my mother back.

In the months following my mother's suicide, I was often only able to lie on my bed sobbing. My mom had taught me how to play and laugh, and now she was telling me that life was not worth living. Hadn't I loved her enough? Was I supposed to save her? At times I could barely hold my head above water with my own problems. How could I have rescued her? Her suicide made me feel that I had failed her. Could I, or someone else, have saved her from her marriage, her sense of isolation, her loss of spirituality?

After Mom's death I was haunted by what her death meant to me. Early on, I felt lost, motherless, and directionless. As time has passed, I realize what a big part of mothering I have missed. I needed a mother, a guide. I missed out on having a role model who could help me find my way in life. Of course, her suicide has made me realize that she was unable to do for herself what I wanted her to assist me in doing.

At first it was all I could do to endure waves of guilt, grief, anger, and sadness. This took a tremendous toll on me and my marriage. On the first anniversary of my mother's death, my husband asked me for a divorce. I realize that my grief about my mother's suicide affected how present I was in my marriage. But as time went on, I began to heal. With the support of therapy, the waves of sadness came further apart. The intense pain began to feel less a part of my life.

It has been fifteen years now since my mother committed suicide. As much as I continue to miss her, there has been relief too. My life has become less of a tightrope walk. I have learned to take care of myself and develop a new life. New caring friendships, a strong spiritual program in Al-Anon, a church, therapy, and work I care about—all have a part in my new life.

I am in my midlife now, and I hope for an old age. After my mother's death, I did research into her younger life. I wanted to know if suicide was "hereditary." Did her suicide mean that I would ultimately commit suicide? How was I going to avoid going down the same path as my mother? I was scared and wanted a different life for myself. Now I am confident that I am making choices that bring health and well-being to my life. Another blessing of midlife is that I no longer feel so unique. I felt isolated when I was one of the few people I knew who had lost a parent, particularly to suicide. Now my friends are beginning to lose their parents, and I am familiar with the stages of their grief.

I still stumble along, but I am learning that the many changes in my life are not all crises.

Marcia Angelos

Marcia Angelos was thirty-one in 1981 when her mother, aged fifty-nine, completed suicide.

Caretaking

The police notified my grandparents about my mother's death first. My grandfather had been particularly close to Mom—everyone knew she had always been his favorite—and he was the one to call me. I was writing a paper so I let the answering machine pick up. "Doug, this is your grandfather. Call me immediately. There's been a tragedy." His voice was flat. I didn't pick up, but I knew something had happened to Mom. If my grandmother or anyone else in Mom's family had died, she would have been the one to call. I went to the window and stared out at the street for a couple of minutes. I felt my heartbeat speeding up, nervous as I thought about what might have happened. I had talked with my mom only three days before, on my twenty-seventh birthday, and she had sounded upbeat. It took me ten minutes to look up my grandparents' number and call. My grandfather answered in the same flat voice, and he told me that she'd killed herself. He broke down after that and handed the phone to my grandmother.

The rest of that day was a blur. I was torn between doing what I had to do in order to join my family in Florida and wanting to crawl into a warm, dark corner and cry until I had no tears left. I was paralyzed by an inexplicable void, an overwhelming emptiness. I'm amazed that I was able to get everything done; I don't remember doing much of it.

One of the most difficult aspects of handling Mom's death was helping my grandparents get through it. Both of them have suffered health problems in recent years, and my mother's entire family was concerned about whether or not they'd be able to take the stress of Mom's suicide. Our grandmother ("Gammy") has always been a practical person and talked about Mom a lot in the weeks after her suicide. She sensed that it would help her work through her grief. Over time, she was able to get back to her regular routine. Our grandfather, on the other hand, took much longer to reconcile himself to the fact that his favorite daughter was gone. My family and I worried about Grandfather's own will to live. We worried that on top of the restrictions caused by illness and recent deaths of friends, the loss of my mother might cause him to harm himself. From the time that my brother, my girlfriend, and I arrived in Florida until the time we left, we tried to make sure that he was never left alone. We also helped my grandmother locate and hide his gun.

After I left Florida, I found myself calling my grandparents every Sunday—the way my mother had done for years. I realized what I was doing a few weeks after leaving Florida, and I debated whether or not I should continue calling. I didn't want it to appear to my grandparents that I was trying to replace Mom—though of course I was trying to help them feel less of a void in their lives, as well as in my own—but at the same time they have become set in their patterns, and I wanted to minimize all disruptions. I called once more on Sunday, but after that I called less regularly so that I could stay in touch without claiming Mom's place. My grandparents and I have returned to the closeness we had when I was much younger—though now we are mutual caretakers.

Mom's death affected my relationship with my brother, too. I think I expected us to grow a lot closer since Mom's death, and that hasn't quite happened. My brother and I have a fine relationship, not rancorous in any way, but it's just not one with regular contact. We talk about once a month, perhaps every other month.

Although our contact remains infrequent, we feel deeply connected—we've weathered Mom's death in a way different from others around us.

We talk when we need to speculate about what might have caused Mom to kill herself. We've both commented on how Mom loved everything that lived. My brother and I sometimes called her "Mrs. Dolittle" because of her propensity to care for needy animals. Once, we shared a one-thousand-square-foot apartment with two dogs, a guinea pig, two cockatiels, seven spice finches, a parakeet, and a dozen or so goldfish, not counting the strays we took in from time to time for a day or so before turning them over to the ASPCA. She wasn't happy unless she had the responsibility of caring for someone or something that needed her. It's unsettling to think that one of the reasons she may have committed suicide was the shift in our dependence upon her. She was proud that we could take care of ourselves, but she might have considered herself worthless because we didn't rely on her as much as we once had. At the same time, I think she had to know that we relied on her in other ways.

Since Mom's suicide, I've tried to play detective in other ways. Sometimes this feels overly intrusive. But it's hard not to question why, not to look for reasons. In a lot of ways, I really don't want to know what she was experiencing. Sometimes trying to think like my mother, to get inside her skull, worries me because I don't want to lose myself or start thinking so much like her that I, too, become suicidal. I sought other clues through the medical examiner's report. As executor of her estate, I received a copy. Reading that was a mixed blessing; it confirmed that she had committed suicide, but it left me with a vivid image of what my mother looked like in death. Sometimes, it's hard to think about her without seeing that image. When my mind inexplicably wanders back to that image, I distract myself. Unfortunately, I haven't done this through my studies. More frequently, I distract myself with a lot of television (which I never used to watch heavily), movies, Internet surfing . . . anything to get my mind off that image.

For me, a potent antidote to this image are the pendants my brother and I had made. We wanted to keep Mom close to us, to do something that would honor her memory and her interests. We had two pendants made, one a yin of yellow gold and the other a yang of white gold, each with some of her ashes sealed inside. In this way, we carry her with us wherever we go. Every day, we remember her. We remember that she gave us life and was — is — an integral part of who we are. We remember that we are her legacy and that there's a bond between us as much as there was between our mother and each of us. She taught us so much — to respect others, to consider the ramifications of our actions, to love rather than to hate or fear. It's sad that she wasn't able to follow the teachings she instilled in us.

I lost my best friend when Mom killed herself, though I don't think I ever told her that when she was alive. At least not in those words. In a lot of ways, she knew me better than anyone does and probably better than anyone will. I hope that she is able to know where I am and how I am, and how much I love her, wherever she is.

Doug Battema

Doug Battema was twenty-seven in 1996 when his mother, aged forty-nine, completed suicide.

The Prodigal Son Diaries

You could set your watch by her Buick. Not once in my mother's decorated tenure as family chauffeur had she ever failed to arrive on schedule. Not in grade school, when her idea of "free time" was the on-the-road calm between Little League drop-offs and piano lesson pick-ups. Not in junior high when, in addition to me, more likely than not she was carting around the rest of my testosterone-addled brood. And not even in high school, after I had missed a ride for some ignominious reason like an after-school detention or for girls with names like Alexis.

Maybe that's why of all the infinite number of things that could have come as a shock that afternoon: the roar of the engine, the intoxicating smell of gas, the frantic pace of rescue personnel, most surprising of all was the incongruity. For the first time in her fifty-five years—at least the portion that I had witnessed—my mother had placed her own needs ahead of her family. I know best, because she staged it that way. Fact or fiction, in the deep of the night when I spring such thoughts from their bell jars, that's the way I spin it: that she knew it would be me; that she recognized the darkness in my soul; that I, better than anyone, would understand. But the moment my eyes fixed on her lifeless body, her legs as long and frozen as ski poles, I died too. Or, more precisely, the selfish me was born. That was three years ago. Or maybe it was a hundred. These days, sometimes it's hard to tell. What I can say for sure is that afternoon, the cries of sirens still tiny in the distance, all time stood still.

I knew right away that something inside had been irretrievably shut down. The forces of repression had attached themselves to my ego like piranha on a drowning sumo wrestler. It's a faint memory now, but I used to care about people. I was well liked.

That was before I closed myself off. Or I was closed off. It's hard to say which. It wasn't anger or guilt or even grief that fueled my emotional meltdown. What I was feeling (or not feeling) was more like a sad hypnosis—like someone had cracked the code to my most secret places and systematically snipped the wiring. I was the walking, waking dead. It would take others longer to see.

At the hospital, my father and I sat wordlessly in the waiting room while doctors with wan eyes and rumpled hair scurried about. They asked if we needed anything. I said no. Dad stepped out to confirm the arrival time of my sister's flight. Smelling a wounded prey, the pastor from my parent's church moved deliberately in my direction. I braced myself for a spiritual litmus test.

"How are you holding up son?" he inquired.

"Hangin' in there," I lied.

"I understand you recently graduated college . . . ."

A laundry list of well-intentioned inquiries ensued. I can't remember what they were exactly. Words were raining like friendly fire, but all I could think about was the size of his hands. He had the kind of magnanimous, oversize paws one would expect for a guy in his line of work. Not that I'd know. I'm not anti-God or anything, I've just never been one for church. But the pastor didn't know this. My parents were new to town. My dad had recently signed on as president of a prominent pharmaceutical company. I felt conspicuous. I took a chance anyway.

"The thing is, Father, I'm not sure what I feel. I mean, I'm not sure I feel anything."

I could see it in his eyes; I had failed. Although he mumbled something reassuring, I knew he didn't understand. That was the first in a long procession of impromptu exams. I flagged them all. That is to say, I wasn't capable of giving people what they wanted.

I wasn't capable of tears. Some told me I was strong. I let myself believe them.

At the funeral, while others were deep in prayer, I kept thinking about *Star Trek*. The one where Mr. Spock dies. Before his dramatic self-sacrifice, in order to gain immortality he impregnates his soul in the body of an unwitting bystander. In the sequel, everyone suspected Captain Kirk, because Spock loved him best. But it turns out it was really Dr. McCoy. He and Spock were more alike than anyone guessed. I wondered if what was growing inside of me were the morose seeds of her Vulcan hand-me-downs. Was *I* depressed? Sure, I'd hit some rough patches before, but I could always explain them away as growing pains. "Don't worry about me," I'd tell my more sympathetic friends.

Like most nubile twentysomethings, I'd endured my share of post-relationship fallout. I was all too familiar with the unshaven, sleep-till-noon, cryin'-in-my-beer lifestyle that accompanies having one's heart broken. Given the circumstances, I'd always thought my proclivity to bouts of darkness was somewhat normal. Truth be told, I secretly took a small measure of pride in my brooding disposition. As an English major, I could appreciate the virtues of a tortured soul. It's what separates the artists from the accountants. But for all my forays into fetal position funks that, by comparison, made Sylvia Plath read like a Cathy comic, somehow this was different. Aside from being born, I did nothing directly to bring this about. Or did I?

As the pastor rose to read from the Good Book, I wondered if I shared more in common with my mother than a set of perfectly formed eyelashes and an affinity for college hoops. I wondered, as I added my raspy baritone to "Amazing Grace," if one day her demons would get the best of me, too. "Oedipus wrecks," I mumbled softly. Nobody noticed.

After the ceremony, we formed a line. It seemed like the thing to do. I strategically sandwiched myself between my uncle and my cousin—talkative chaps both. The melancholy procession began. I could feel the wagons circling around my heart. As friends and well-wishers inched their way in my direction, I tried to avoid making eye contact. Their presence was comforting to be sure, I just didn't know what to say. "Thanks for being here" became my mantra. They told me to seek out a therapist. It was their conversational crutch. "It really helps to talk to someone about what you are feeling," they advised. I didn't have the strength to argue. I went to assuage their worries. I went for them.

"How's your father holding up?" the doctor asked. "He's doing a helluva job with that company." I felt conspicuous. I sat slope-shouldered in my chair while he looked over my file. As my eyes moved in increasingly larger concentric circles around the room, it occurred to me that the artifice of my immediate surroundings seemed more akin to a late-night talk show set than what I had expected to find in a shrink's office.

The doctor was surprisingly small. Like a Tolkien character. He was dressed casually: loafers, tattered khaki pants, and no tie. A pair of dark-rimmed Buddy Holly glasses sat perched atop an enormous nose. In place of a well-kept white beard—a look that I had erroneously assumed to be requisite for all practicing psychiatrists—was a jet-black David Niven mustache. He spoke in a folksy manner without the slightest hint of a German accent.

"It says here that you are a movie buff (I was asked to list my hobbies). What's your favorite genre?" he asked.

"I like Hitchcock," I said. "I just rented *The Lady Vanishes*." My face flared about a bizzillion shades of red as the irony struck me. My one therapeutic epiphany. It was lost on him. I brought him up to speed on the particulars.

"We learned of her depression about six months ago." He took copious notes. Occasionally he looked up to give me a benevolent nod.

"Was she on any medication?"

"Prozac didn't work for her. Neither did shock therapy. I know she was taking something, but I'm not sure what. I'll ask my dad."

"Yes, ask your dad. How's he holdin' up by the way? He's done a helluva job with that company."

For three sessions, after laying bare the details of her illness, he played witness for the prosecution while I cross-examined my childhood. Like a Jackson Browne ballad stuck on auto-reverse, I bent his ear on everything from lost loves to lost puppies. But instead of giving myself over to the therapeutic process, I was more intent on dazzling him with my analytic acumen. I doled out such pearls of self-awareness as "Sometimes, I just try to remind myself of what Nietzsche said. You know, 'that which does not kill me can only make me stronger.' Actually in my case it's more like 'that which does not kill me can only give me really bad hair.'"

"And how does that make you feel?" he inquired.

"How does what make me feel? How does my hair make me feel?"

"Well, has your hair loss caused you to experience any untoward emotions?" As the words left his mouth, an unconscious hand excused itself from his side and began to scratch the back nine of a well-coifed, but thinning, mane.

"Hmm. I guess it makes me feel . . . I dunno. Bald?" I said phrasing an unfortunate statement of fact in the form of a question.

His face was expressionless. Like an elementary school teacher at the blackboard waiting for the class to "settle down."

Much to my chagrin, no deep seated angst was set free in these therapy sessions. Nor were any life-altering revelations offered up. Eighty bucks an hour and I'd learned more about myself from a fortune cookie. Of course, I didn't tell him about the dreams. Or maybe they hadn't started yet. He said I should come back in a month. I lied and said I would.

I don't blame the doctors. Hers or mine. Like my mother, I, too, could play hide-and-seek with my blue demons, the ones she bequeathed to me. Besides, there's only so much help you can give to someone who is not willing to help himself first (aforementioned fortune cookie wisdom).

My mother hid her wounds so well and for so long that in the end they simply collapsed and swallowed her whole. Mom even fooled the pros. A couple years before her death she was diagnosed with everything from Lyme disease to Rocky Mountain spotted fever. Later on, through the clarity of hindsight, they guessed that she had probably been masking her depression for some time. Maybe even years. Like her family, it never occurred to the doctors that someone as well-off as she was could feel "blue." Why should she? From all appearances she had it made: a former schoolteacher turned philanthropist in the mornings, doting mother of two by day, corporate cocktail party charmer by night. She waltzed through the well choreographed routine of her day. Mom knew how to work a room. Save a handful of weeks before her death, nobody, not even her children, suspected anything. Aside from the doctors, Dad was her sole confidant.

In retrospect, it's hard to comprehend how naive I was about the whole thing. I actually believed that one day Mom would snap out of her malaise, as if it were simply a matter of will. I convinced myself that what she was going through was just some sort of prolonged empty-nester thing. It was more difficult to rationalize her appearance. I told myself that her extra weight was simply a telltale reminder of holiday excess. Had I not smelled the booze, I might have believed it. But for a while anyway, my sister and I played into her thinly veiled cover-ups. What else could we do? She was seeing a psychiatrist. She was taking medication. From our perspective, it didn't help anything to confront her. After all, my family, Mom included, was anything but confrontational. We needed help, but out of respect for my mother, we decided the best help we could give her was to respect her privacy. Slowly, as time wore on, her facade began to crack and chip away. Lying to others had been easy. It was lying to her that broke my heart. I wanted so much to reach out to her. But how?

Sometimes, during my lunch hour, I'd stop by unannounced to check up on her. I confess with a certain measure of guilt that my visits were motivated by something more than love—I stopped by to chow. I can't say for sure, but I think my lunchtime appearances provided her with an unthreatening sense of purpose. It was as if they momentarily jump-started her dormant maternal instincts. On many occasions, and much to my delight, she served up the most improbable lunchtime fare for her famished twenty-three-year-old little boy.

"Cocoa Vaughn?" I inquired. "Non, non, mon ami. Zis, is zee *coq au vin*," she gently corrected in her best ersatz French.

On these days, lost in the bliss of such culinary delights, I'd forget about the pain and the guilt. All the baggage was temporarily shelved beneath the capacious landscape that is my gut. But before long, even cooking became too much. The gourmet repast gave way to bologna and a note. "Out running errands" or something to that effect. I knew that she was locked away upstairs somewhere. All the same, I pretended not to notice that her Lexus was still in the garage.

It's hard to remember a life without the dreams. They've become so much a part of my nocturnal habits that I've come to accept their inevitability. I regard them now in much the same way I view, say, the act of nighttime flossing: a mostly unpleasant, if not painful, experience, but necessary for long-term health.

While the form is in constant flux, the scenario is always the same. It's late afternoon; I'm on my lunch break. I pull up a serpentine driveway, and for reasons not clearly defined, an indescribable coldness washes over me. As I turn my key in the front door lock, a pungent odor permeates my senses. I think to myself, they must be having some painting done. I call out, but the only response is the hollow echo of my own voice. My steps are slow-motion heavy as I walk through the entry hall, past the family room, past the kitchen, until I come upon a door.

What happens next is never quite the same. Sometimes, I'm the size of an action figure eyeing up an enormous passageway. Other times, like a postmodern Alice, I'm T-rex tall, only the door I'm facing is normal size. But without exception, my hand trembles on the knob, not just because of the adrenaline—the Surround Sound roar of the engine is vibrating the lock. I hesitate. I can feel the hair on the back of my neck standing at attention. If ever there was a defining moment, it's now. "It's just a dream," an unseen narrator whispers in my ear. As I awaken—or more precisely, am awakened by Amy, my wife—the sound of my own cries are still faintly audible in the room.

One thing Freud was right about was the notion that we seek out a mate who reminds us of our parents. Amy only met my mother once. In the cosmic scheme of things, it was enough.

Amy, then just a close college friend, was flying in for New Year's weekend to meet and, ostensibly, party with my parents. She had no idea that the day before, my sister and I had learned for the first time about Mom's illness. I prepared myself for an awkward weekend. A funny thing happened on the way to denial. As soon as she arrived, everything, at least momentarily, was back to normal. My mother, as far as appearances go, was her old self again: quick to laugh, even quicker to bust my chops. We stayed up into the wee hours of the night listening to Mom tell long-winded anecdotes about former babysitters turned asylum residents. A mere coincidence I say. Later on, I confided in Amy. Since that day she has been my best friend. Aside from family, there were times that she was my only friend. I know Mom loved her too. Watching the two of them converse that night, no one would have mistaken them for kin. But if anyone could have looked into their eyes, into their souls, they would have found an identical pair of oversized hearts. Freud was a genius.

Long before the dreams subside, the sympathy dries up. Just like that, without prior warning, you find yourself cut off. And you never even knew you were addicted. Invariably, you watch helplessly as one by one they come to their own inner crossroads. Some get there faster than others, but sooner or later they all get there. They have come to this confluence of paths to debate and ponder your future in their lives. They assume that because they no longer feel the heaviness, the sting, and the fallout of her death, that it's time for you to move on as well. What they don't understand is that asking you to forget about her death is like asking you to deny your legs in favor of flying. No matter how mundane, her death underpins your every movement. But you don't get a vote. You simply watch as they choose one of the three inner paths that lie before them.

Option #1: Due to the tragic circumstances involved, I find the defendant not guilty of selfish behavior in the first degree, and hereby pardon him of any wrongdoing.

In short, people who choose this path are too good for this earth. Priests and grandmothers and the like.

Option #2: Due to a series of unreturned phone calls, moodiness, and being an all-around pain in the ass, I find the defendant guilty of the crime of selfishness in the first degree, and hereby sentence him to remain in the self-imposed exile he began sometime ago.

In short, these people either love you way too much for their own good or never really loved you at all. It's hard to say which.

While some pick a path and never look back, more likely than not, most choose to elect the convenience of a third choice.

Option #3: Due to the tragic circumstances involved, I find the defendant not guilty of the crime of selfishness in the first degree, even though he's a moody pain in the ass and won't return my calls.

In short, it is the travelers of this path that probably love you the most.

I was tired and run down. I hadn't been sleeping well. But above all, I was unusually sad. As a graduate student, this state is pretty much par for the course. Was I depressed? Or was I merely stressed about midterms? The answer wouldn't come for another year.

At some point, I can't say exactly when, somewhere around the time I began to prepare for my MA final exams, I had my answer. The difference between depression and grief? Time. It was hard to believe, but for the first time in months, things were going my way. I was on the brink of finishing my degree. I was three months away from marriage. And I'd rekindled many of the friendships I'd let slip away. If I didn't know any better, I would have described myself as, well, content.

While Mom's death is an undeniable presence at almost every major life event, it's the little ones that get to me most. I drove by a kindergarten recently. I watched as a group of kids were enveloped in the love of the after-school rides that awaited them. For the first

time in years, I wept. I smiled to myself, and I glanced at my watch
to be sure. What I had suspected was true. That afternoon, for one
fleeting moment, all time stood still. And as I made my way back
home, time was all I could think about. Time and *Star Trek*. The
one where Mr. Spock dies.

Todd Tobias

Todd Tobias was twenty-three in 1993 when his
mother, aged fifty-five, completed suicide.

Crossroads

With the exception of my father (who died in a car accident when I was an infant), everyone in my immediate family has died by suicide. There's no way fully to understand what would drive a person to suicide, and the cases of my brother and mother are no exceptions.

On Easter Sunday 1986, when I was sixteen years old, I was informed that my older brother was dead by suicide. This news followed days of uncertainty as to his whereabouts. Although I'd suspected throughout the search that he would be found dead, I was surprised that he'd killed himself. To this day, it remains unclear what factors brought him to such a desperate act. Many rumors circulated through our small community. Many theories were floated. I cannot claim to know why he took his life. I dealt with Bob's death with the most damaging methods available to me: alcohol and marijuana. Being an epileptic, such behavior was more harmful to my health than it was to the other mixed-up kids I ran around with. Psychologists would argue that chemical abuse itself is a form of attempted suicide. I didn't see it that way—I didn't want to die; I just wanted to avoid the pain in my life.

Despite my drinking, and over one hundred unexcused absences, I managed to squeak through my senior year with a 2.5 GPA, which was just enough to get me admitted to Eastern Oregon State College in the fall of 1987. I registered as a business student, but my true major was still "recreational chemicals." Given the emotional pressures in my life, my academic performance that year was less than stellar. By spring term, although I had sobered up, I was on academic probation. That term, I registered for "Introduction to Expository Writing," a course required for graduation. But I found the first assignment impossible to do, and I dropped the class. The assignment? To write an essay about myself. My paralysis in the face of that topic opened my eyes to my fear of revealing to the world that I'd lost someone to suicide. The stigma of Bob's self-murder drove me out of college. Soon I began drinking again.

I found a job with a local janitorial service and worked there for a couple of years until my boss grew tired of my destructive behavior. Employment problems prompted me to attend a couple of Alcoholics Anonymous meetings. These helped me find the courage to begin the long journey to sobriety, but I could never bring myself to share my loss with others. Suicide was a taboo subject in my community and it seemed utterly inappropriate to reveal my brother's suicide — even to a group offering unconditional support.

In the months before my mom died, I was still drinking occasionally, but it was not nearly as bad as it had been. I was working part-time for a rancher and making plans to return to college in the fall to pick up where I left off after Bob's death. Going back to school was a chance for me to start over, to put my past behind me, and to focus on my future. I made it a point to stop by Mom's house every day to check on her. She continued to struggle with physical and emotional problems, but overall, she was doing well. She was involved in various activities, and the mental illness that had plagued her was being held at bay. Growing up, there were a lot of things that Mom couldn't handle that became my responsibility (grocery shopping, paying bills, balancing the checkbook, house cleaning, minor repairs, etc.), and checking in on her was just an extension of this relationship.

She was very agitated over a minor financial matter the last time I saw her, but I wasn't overly concerned. I was confident her mood would pass before the night was over. When repeated phone calls to her the next day went unanswered, I began to worry. At the first opportunity, I jumped in a pickup truck and went over to her house. There I discovered her lifeless body and empty bottles of pills.

People's response to Mom's suicide was less hysterical than it was to my brother's—and more upsetting to me. Her death was as tragic as Bob's, but few people treated it that way. It's true that she had a lot of problems, but it was not her time to go. Given the difficulties of her life, many accepted her death as if it were some kind of "rational suicide." At the funeral, she was eulogized as a woman who wasn't afraid of death, "Bon voyage, Donna! You got what you wanted . . . hope you're happy!" It made me sick that people talked about what a wonderful lady Mom was and then calmly discussed her death as a justifiable decision. For me, it was not. In my grief, I started drinking heavily again.

After Mom's death, the distance between my aunt and uncle and me increased rapidly. I didn't like the way they accepted her death as though it was inevitable, and I noticed they were avoiding me. Did they think it was my fault? Were they waiting for me to kill myself—"Bob and Donna are gone, I wonder what Tom's going to do for his fifteen minutes of fame?" To be perfectly honest, I fear one of them to be next or one of my cousins. My aunt only recently revealed to me that before I was born two other members of our family took their own lives. I'm afraid of having kids because at some point, they will ask about their grandma and their uncle. It's a troublesome legacy to pass on to another generation. I want to talk more with my aunt, but this is a sensitive area and it seems to be off-limits.

About two months after Mom's suicide, her best friend took her life as well. That prompted me to look into counseling because I was afraid that this suicide thing might turn out to be "contagious." My brother, my mother, her best friend . . . who was next? I felt like I was walking around with a big X on my forehead, a sign that I was doomed. Therapy made me even more confused. I wanted to talk about the suicides in my life, but the counselors were more interested in dispensing lithium than helping me work through my grief. In this respect, the counselors were cut from the same cloth as the rest of my community. No one wants to hear my witness to the effects of suicide in my life.

On my own, I'm moving ahead. In December of 1994, I stopped drinking completely, and I've stayed sober since then. I'm considering going back to college, but the prospect scares me. I don't want to be faced with another class in which I am asked to write an essay about my life and share it with a bunch of kids I hardly know. Nor do I wish to have to rely on school counselors for support—when I went in for help after Bob's death, one of them began to cry. Meeting people is very difficult because typically family is the first thing people ask about, and it is the last subject I want to cover. I'm at a point in my life at which I'm trying to understand what happened to my family. I'm looking for a way to integrate it into my life and move into a happier future.

Tom Dalton

Tom Dalton was twenty-two in 1991 when his mother, aged fifty-two, completed suicide.

Range of Vision

As the ten-year anniversary of my mother's suicide approaches, the event that was so intense, so meaningful, has eroded into an oddity to be shared at random intervals with new acquaintances. Many of the circumstances surrounding her depression and eventual suicide have become a cloudy mix of memories and muddled time lines, but as I grasp to keep her alive in my mind, I have come to realize that the years leading up to her suicide may have had more impact on me than the act itself. While there is no denying that her self-imposed exposure to carbon monoxide in our Akron, Ohio, garage was a tragic ending to a several-year saga of hospitals, psychiatrists, and overwhelming sadness, my vision of her illness had already been altered to the point that her death brought a sense of relief. As a teenager, I spent many hours comforting my mother in her depression. I have countless memories of her crying on my shoulder, sobbing about how sorry she was or how much she loved me. And I cried too. But I also developed a bigger view, an ability to see her sorrow with the correct perspective. It was her sorrow . . . not mine.

I suppose my mother's death has changed me, but it's difficult to specify how. Since I've spent the majority of my adult life without her, it is hard to imagine how things would be different if she were still alive. I think living in the midst of her bouts with depression did more to shape who I am today than that she committed suicide. Through this unsolicited exposure, I learned to cherish the moments when she felt good, to understand that life can be overwhelming, and that mental illness is a powerful force. By the time she succeeded in ending her misery, I had resigned myself to the fact that she would probably take her own life. Yet when informed of her death, I instantly wept. I was fortunate to have an immediate understanding of why she had ended her life; still the knowledge that she was truly gone struck hard.

Between all of the treatments, recoveries, and relapses, my mother had become just a shell of the woman I grew up knowing. Her soul had been hollowed out, and her obsessions had overtaken her life. To have seen her continue her downward spiral would have, most likely, been far more difficult to experience than her death. Her act was a way to save us, as unfortunate as that may sound, and I know that's why she did it. To her troubled mind, she was making the ultimate sacrifice for the good of her family. She could not see her positive qualities; she could only see the trouble that she had brought. Of course, one could view her suicide as selfish. I can't say that her timing was the best, particularly since my sister, just shy of her eighteenth birthday, was the one to discover her. However, I cannot say that anything my mother did was intentionally selfish. She did what she thought was necessary. Who am I to say that she was wrong? It was her life . . . and it was her death.

At first, my mother's act seemed like an inseparable part of my being: "If you want to know me, it's important that you know this . . . ." And, I must admit, I basked in the glory of my tragedy to a certain extent. Enduring a parental suicide garners a great deal of attention, and it was the perfect event for my existential leanings. It's nearly impossible to find anything more absurd than the person who helped give you life taking her own. I wanted everyone to know about my mother's death. I wanted to show how strong I was, how together, how mature. My determination to earn the respect of those around me gave me strength to deal with her loss. To this day, it is still a bit of information that I like to share with people. There is a certain amount of power—and comfort—to be gained from showing others our battle scars from life. As time has passed, it has become less difficult to disassociate my mother's act from my life.

Following her death, my family divided up her album collection, and I acquired her James Taylor records. That summer, to a great extent out of respect, I attended one of his concerts. I knew that if my mother had been alive and healthy, she would have wanted to go. At that concert I was struck with the overwhelming desire to play guitar. Less than three months later I had written my first song, about her, and had found a way to voice my emotions and work through much of my pain and questioning. My guitar became my counselor, and I consulted with it regularly.

One of the more troubling results of my mother's suicide is that my wife never knew my mother and now only has confusing pictures of who she was. I know it confounds her to this day and is, at best, an insoluble puzzle that might shed some light on who I am. Suicide may be unique in the way that it seems so foreign, so mysterious. Death by natural causes or even by accidents is somehow cleaner, less messy. Death by suicide leaves many unanswerable questions. How crazy was she? Could the death have been prevented? Are the feelings that brought about the death inheritable? How could she do it? Questions I have long since given up answering will always remain for my wife.

Another unfortunate circumstance of my mother's death was my family's inability to celebrate the life that she did lead. It was difficult to honor the life of someone who had chosen to end it prematurely. When the immediate family gathered the morning after the death, we all were determined to get the service over with and move on. We did not feel it was appropriate to linger over the tragedy of her act. Less than three days after she was discovered in the garage, we were all back to our lives. Though we grieved in our own ways, it was difficult to grieve together.

My father and I discussed the suicide extensively during the year that followed, for he fell into a deep depression himself not long after her death. As I visited him in the hospital, he shared with me his own thoughts of suicide. I quickly knew what to say: "Go ahead." I didn't have the patience to go through another sequence of extended counseling sessions. My ability to commiserate with the emotions of my parents had reached its limit. I lashed out at him, saying that if he wanted to end it, he should get it over with because it was fair neither to him nor to me to go through all this again. I understood his sorrow and feelings of confusion, but I was given the opportunity to say to him what I suppose I would like to have said to my mother: "Don't you want to see your kids get married? Aren't you interested in the twists and turns of life? Don't you have any desire to see the mysteries of our existence continue to unfold? Don't you want to have a chance to see your grandchildren?" He patiently listened to my monologue, and I went home. As I drove away from the hospital I felt a little guilty, but mostly I was relieved that I had spoken my mind without hesitation. He soon left the hospital, returned to work, and got on with his life. Whether or not my words helped him turn the corner on his depression is inconsequential. My choice to express my feelings honestly and without censure liberated me from his pain and helped me deal with mine.

My sister and I talked a great deal about the death, and we continue to discuss it to this day. Whenever one of us has a particularly troubling dream or memory, we instantly call the other. Our shared experience has served as a point of reference for a relationship that had not yet fully developed at the time of the suicide. My sister has become a wonderful confidante and friend. My brother, three years my senior, and I have not yet fully hashed out our feelings about the suicide. I have tried to broach the subject occasionally, but it never seems to take hold of our conversation. I often feel he has been isolated from the healing process because he has lived away from the rest of us even before the suicide. In the past year or so, we have begun to grow closer, however, and I am confident we will have the opportunity to discuss everything further in the near future.

One of the challenges in writing this essay was separating my family's tragedy from those that every family must face. Soon after the suicide, my father and I were eating at a restaurant, and my mind was adrift with thoughts of "Where do we go from here?" when from the booth behind me, I overheard people who were also dealing with loss. Apparently a member of their family had recently died, and they were quietly consoling each other. Suddenly, I came to the realization that, though I felt isolated from the rest of humanity, thousands of people were that very day dealing with losses of their own. Sure, not all of the deaths were suicides, but people were grieving all the same. It became obvious that I was not alone.

As I grow older, I am even more convinced that part of the human experience is dealing with unfortunate events that leave us confused and empty. I overcame my need to feel sorry for myself by developing the ability to frame my tragedy in a more universal context. After my mother's death I had a tendency to see my life as a movie, of which I was the star. Everything was about me, and all of the people with whom I came into contact were nothing more than supporting players. In my movie, I expected everything to relate to me and my concerns and feelings. What I have come to realize is that I am simply a member of a worldwide supporting cast for everyone else. There are no stars. We are all faced with success and failure, triumph and tragedy, life and death. Our goal, therefore, should not be to wallow in our individual losses or bask in our victories, but to refocus our attention on the bigger picture: We are faced with one precious life, one chance to live out a series of minutes, hours, days. . . . Yes, my mother's suicide was an intense event in mine; however, as many of you who are reading this book can confirm, I was not and am not alone. We are all dealing with tragedy.

Exposure to my mother's illness and suicide taught me that life is something to be maneuvered. When an obstruction is reached, another path must be chosen. The possibilities for change and growth are limitless if one is open and willing. This lesson has served me well in relationships, career decisions, and my everyday life. After witnessing my mother's inability to change things she did not like, I have become aware of the power that I do hold. I can change things. When opportunities arise, I am more likely to take advantage. When chances to expand my horizon are within reach, I quickly grab on. When life throws punches, I have developed the ability to dodge instead of take them face first.

My mother was a wonderful woman to everyone but herself. Her caring devotion to her fellow man and selfless ability to love still inspire me. There's no doubt that witnessing that kind of concern for others left a considerable impression on my life. My decision to enter the ministry is a product of that influence. In the fall of 1997, I entered seminary to prepare for life as a Unitarian/Universalist minister. My ministry will expand my mother's tender influence to countless others.

Of course it is tragic that this woman would want to end her life, but it was her decision to make. Of course I wish that she were still here . . . to welcome me home, to meet my wife, to be my mom, but she chose her path, and that path is unalterable. Am I angry? Only occasionally. I am mostly disappointed that she found suicide to be the best alternative to her pain. My mother chose to die, but she lives on regardless. That is the power of her life that will never be relinquished.

Mark Stringer

Mark Stringer was twenty-one in 1988 when his mother, aged forty-seven, completed suicide.

Grandchildren

I know my father felt shame about his father's suicide. I was not honestly informed of my grandfather's death until I was eighteen; then I was asked not to tell anyone, but to lie and say he died of a heart attack. Since my father's death, I have vowed to be honest in order to prevent further shame. As my child to be grows, I will be truthful about his or her grandfather's life and death. I will explain his disease (bipolar disorder), the reasons as I know them (financial pressures and inability to share feelings), and the method (a gun).

Carrie P. Riley

My baby girl is now thirteen months old and, if all goes well, will be joined by a sibling next June. Once while cleaning my mother's house, I found stacks of books, toys, and stuffed animals she had bought for the "grandchildren." Anger rises when I think "she should be here"—for my little girl, for me. I will tell my children the truth but at what age, I'm not sure. Before that time, I will share lots of pictures, letters, and memories. This will allow me to introduce adult topics gradually as my children grow older.

Margo McDaniel

One of the most painful tasks of my journey to recovery has been wrestling with what to tell my children about their grandfather, a man they never knew. How could I tell my children this horrible truth about suicide and how it devastated my life? At the age of five, my oldest child asked about my father and how he died. I found it too difficult to tell the truth so I said it was an accident. When this child was in high school, he told me of a friend whose brother had completed suicide; I knew it was time to tell them the truth. When I told my two oldest children, ages fifteen and ten, they cried as did I. My youngest child was told this past summer at the age of eleven. My siblings, too, have told their children when they felt it was time.

Susan Ford

Suicide as Family Destiny?

Suicide is a two-, possibly three-, generation pattern in my family. I now live in fear that this "tradition" will continue. I know
that I am at risk. Since I have felt suicidal once, I know that I must
be conscious of my feelings, not bury them, in order to prevent my
own suicide. I am also concerned about my two brothers' risk of
suicide. I believe that if I continue to be honest with myself and
others I will decrease my risk for suicide and hopefully stop the
family tradition.

I will never forget the moment I felt suicidal. I was sitting alone
by a pool. Thoughts came of how to drown myself—such odd
thoughts for a good swimmer. "No one will miss me. My family will
be fine. My husband of three months will move on with his life and
remarry." I was so angry and sad that I wanted to relieve my pain.
When I realized that these were dangerous thoughts, I immediately
called my counselor for an emergency visit. I learned that my overwhelming pain was from anger I stored up about my father's suicide
and the abandonment that this made me feel.

Carrie P. Riley

For a long time my father's suicide was a family secret kept from his
grandchildren, and it might have stayed that way until one nephew
experienced depression. This greatly frightened his mother. She
told her son about our father and was able to get him some help.
My sister's fear is one all of my siblings live with, wondering if one
of us or our children will fall victim to suicide. As my thirty-ninth
birthday approached, I wondered if I too would succumb to depression and suicide. I compared myself to my father; I looked for
similar traits or signs and found some. I could be demanding, was

easily depressed, and was dissatisfied with my life. I also worried about my siblings and wondered if one of them might consider suicide.

Susan Ford

II

Loss of a Father

Old at Heart

When I first learned of my father's suicide, I cried because he would never walk me down the aisle at my wedding, and he would never know my future children. I cried because I felt he didn't care enough to stay alive for me, his daughter, his flesh and blood. I cried because he seemed not to care about what this would do to me. I cried because we had so much unfinished business. I cried because I felt so utterly alone.

Now almost a year later, I have gone from a happy-go-lucky recent college graduate, a young twenty-something just starting out in life, to an expert on death, funeral parlors, coffins, cremation, grieving, suicide, therapy, manic depression, elder care, lawyers, medical negligence, accountants, money management, mutual funds, real estate, and taxes. At the ripe old age of twenty-three, I am confronted with problems typically associated with midlife. While most of my friends are either still receiving checks from their fathers, living in their father's houses, or being walked down the aisle by their fathers, I now own half of both my dad's house and condo, and I am landlord to tenants three times my age. Just today, while on the phone with my sister for the fourth time this week regarding my paternal grandmother's income tax extension, I heard myself saying, "I am growing very tired of taking responsibility," for the life and death of my father, the life of my eighty-five-year-old grandmother, and the needs of my heartsick mother. More and more, I feel as though I have adopted three very needy children as a result of my father's act.

Although my mother and I have not shut each other out completely since my father's death, we've definitely had more downs than ups in our relationship. At first, my mother was a harbor in a storm. The day after Dad died, she hugged me and whispered, "I know you aren't all right, so I won't even ask you." I still consider that the wisest thing anyone has said to me. (Especially in comparison to some of the lines I've heard—I have to watch myself not to respond to "It really threw me for a loop," with "Yeah, no kidding, you're not half as thrown as I am, buddy.") Before my father killed himself, my mother and I were allies dealing with a father who was very controlling of family finances, despite my parents' divorce twelve years before. Now, having my father's estate split between my sister and me has created new tensions. I feel guilty that Mom raised us without Dad's financial support, and now I have his money. My mother is very upset about this situation, and she maintains that my sister and I owe her this money. This reversal of financial power has injected an ugly dimension in our family dynamic.

My sister and I have picked up our relationship where we left off when our parents divorced. We talk regularly, mostly about the house and the money rather than about our personal struggles. Sometimes, however, we do share our feelings in an effort to determine whether our separate experiences contain common features. As we recognize common emotional bonds, we are drawn closer together.

Throughout this ordeal, my mother's family has been very supportive of my sister and me. Perhaps because of this, I want to live closer to them. I had considered such a move before, but now I am acting on it. This move will also put me in closer proximity to my grandmother, for whom I am now a principal caretaker. With the responsibility of my grandmother, I have become knowledgeable about elder care matters that most people are forced to deal with when they are in their forties or fifties. I have a lot in common with older people now and sometimes dismiss my peer group's concerns as trivial.

Given the dramatic changes in my life over the past year, I have developed a strong need to live in the present. The future is so unpredictable. I am more inclined to do things, *now*. I didn't wait to buy the convertible I have wanted since high school, or to get the dog I had wanted, or to travel. I do hold myself back from getting married however. Although emotionally I feel ready to be married to my boyfriend, I never want there to be any suspicion that I got married because of my father's suicide. Earlier this year, my sister decided to get married, and I just dread seeing all our family and friends at the wedding, including my dad's, there without him. The void where he should be will be so large.

My dad always told me that "when you're young, you don't sweat the small stuff." But I have come to realize that life is too short and I am old in spirit. I sweat all the stuff, not necessarily by choice.

Heather Zuzick

Heather Zuzick was twenty-two in 1995 when her father, aged nearly fifty-four, completed suicide.

Growing toward the Light

I

Dad was my model of emotional strength, and I respected his know-how when it came to practical matters. From the many stories he told came a wonderful sense of history: accounts of Gandhi from what he'd read in the original news clippings, his own memories of the Great Depression, World War II, the Civilian Conservation Corps, presidential races, local history. He also had a great sense of local geography. He gave directions according to dead snags, clearings, and creeks. I spent my childhood growing up in the woods outside of town. It was a slice from the original homestead that belonged to my dad's parents. Dad wasn't much on having a "modern home." He figured he was doing darn good because he could "do it himself." Kerosene lamps and wood heat were our daily fare. Every summer we were sure to be kept busy cutting firewood. We depended on it. We did have indoor plumbing and a party-line phone. Two rings was our ring.

Dad had already raised a daughter who was now grown with kids of her own. He was divorced and had adopted us when he and Mom were married. He was a quiet man, not given to sharing much about his personal feelings. Conversation was viewed as a waste of time. An exception was his occasional story telling. I remember him saying, "Talking doesn't get the work done." A lot of what I learned came from doing chores, lots of them. Chores weren't measured in terms of hours, but in terms of completing the chore. Often we spent days doing a chore until it was completed. It wouldn't make sense to measure the work in terms of hours. There wasn't such a thing as an eight-hour day. My upbringing in many ways was like the nineteenth century, even though it was during the 1960s and 1970s.

I felt such a deep gratitude that Dad adopted me as his own child. This gratitude wasn't dampened by the mistakes he made as a parent or by his suicide. Looking back, I hope Dad knew just how much I loved him and how deeply I appreciated knowing him as a father. Feelings such as these were not expressed in my youth. In the years to follow, mentioning these feelings to Dad would cause him discomfort, and so I left the rest unspoken. I didn't always understand him or his reasons for doing the things he did. I am doing my best to honor him by understanding his upbringing and what that means. I loved Dad dearly and could not have loved him more had he been my father from birth. He was my dad.

Mom and Dad divorced after twenty-seven years of marriage, which was painful for me even though I was an adult. I was able to work through it and was determined to keep both parents in my life. Dad was depressed and lonely, but he seemed to be managing it well. Although I worried about his health, he was doing things he hadn't done in years. I felt relieved.

II

It was three years after the divorce and just two weeks before we were to go to see Dad for a visit. My children were excited and already planning what they would do once they got to Grandpa's. They wanted to see Blackjack, Grandpa's black Lab. They wanted to run through the "camp" and across the dam on Dad's property. They wanted to sit on Grandpa's bulldozer and ride in his truck. They wanted Grandpa to cook them breakfast on the wood stove.

On August 18, 1992, the phone rings at 6:00 a.m. I am still in bed. The answering machine comes on, and I hear my brother-in-law David's voice, "Wanda, if you're home pick up the phone." I can tell he is crying and something is terribly wrong. My first thought is of my sister Joanne. I'm feeling scared and wondering how to prepare for whatever news is coming. I pick up the phone. I'm sitting on the edge of my bed. "Hello. This is Wan . . . ." David breaks in, "I'm sorry we didn't call you last night, but . . . ." My thoughts are racing. It's not Joanne, he said "we," so who is it? What's happened? David continues, "but we just couldn't make the call. We have some really bad news. Dad died last night."

I am stunned, shocked. I had just spoken to him the day before yesterday or so. He seemed fine. Then I remind myself about Joanne telling me he had been worrying about things that hadn't really happened. He had said people were spying on him and were going to take him off his land. Years ago he had mentioned he wanted to die at home and not anywhere else. The fear of being removed from his home would be a tremendous stress for him. There were other things happening that were very stressful for Dad. I was concerned. I was glad we would be seeing him in two weeks . . . and now I am being told time has run out.

David explains that they went to check on Dad. He explains between sobs the circumstances of Dad's death. I am numb. I can't believe this is happening! Everything is going in slow motion, and in a strange way, somehow like a mime, like a silent movie. The only things racing are the questions I have. I can't bring myself to ask them all. I tell myself I could get the answers later if they really mattered. David tells me, "He didn't feel any pain. He knew what he wanted." But I can't comprehend all this. I keep replaying in my mind what Dad must have done that day before he died—what he was thinking and feeling just before he died. I want to reach out and stop it from happening, but it's already done.

The drive from Oregon to my childhood home was a long one. We did our best to enjoy it. We stopped in the Redwood National Park and let the boys enjoy the huge trees, the ferns, and the mossy forest floor. While they were busy exploring, I was remembering all the times I had spent with Dad in these redwood forests. It wasn't the same now.

When we arrived in town I went to Dad's place. I had to be there. I had to see for myself. I had to "talk to Dad." The drive from town was a road that ran back to my childhood. The road was the same. No improvements. Sometimes it seemed a short seven miles, other times it seemed like a long way. This afternoon it was long.

We approached the bottom of the hill. As I drove up the hill, I felt every bump in the road, every bump over the ditches to drain off the water. I tried to feel it as it felt to Dad. I tried to think his thoughts as he drove up this hill. I tried to see what caught his attention. We passed the bulldozer on which I had spent many hours sitting next to Dad as he moved the earth to make new roads. New roads for firewood. The house came into view. . . . I caught my breath, quietly, hoping no one would notice us. I didn't want to explain anything. I didn't want any questions.

We said hello to the dog, Blackjack, who was chained near the house. I walked around. I listened to the dirt move underfoot as I walked, and I wondered how it sounded under the weight of Dad's foot. It took some time before I could walk up the steps. I wondered if they creaked liked that for Dad, and I unlocked the door. I didn't know what to expect. I didn't know what I would feel going in this house, or what I would see. A house made by Joanne and David and Dad . . . It was warm and had linoleum floors—a change from the cold concrete of his old place. A house he could walk in barefooted when he was old.

The boys were anxious to run and play with Blackjack. The situation was not one they could relate to yet. I was thankful they were so young and innocent. The worry of how we would work through this in the years to come, especially their adolescent years, flashed through my mind.

III

As I walked through Dad's house, I went slowly. The stillness and quiet were overwhelming. Tears welled up in my eyes and spilled over. This place would never know his presence again. More painful still, I wouldn't know his presence in this place anymore. I saw the dishes he used at his last meal. I imagined him sitting in the chair at the end of the table. I noticed the kerosene lamp that should have been lit, and I saw his eyeglasses. I stood and took in the silence. I looked at the canned food on the shelves and the items on the countertops. I started a fire in the wood stove one last time.

I would never have taken the luxury of looking at Dad's things so carefully when he was living. Respecting people's privacy was ingrained in me as a child. Going through people's things was considered disrespectful, but then it was the only way I could be with him. Items that I had considered trivial became important. What kind of can opener did Dad like best? Did he look out the window when he ate? What did he see? Seeking the answers to these questions was my way of still being with Dad. I didn't want him to be gone. I didn't want him to be dead. "This just can't be!" I thought to myself. I felt that thought in my stomach. "How can I live the rest of my life without Dad?" I couldn't imagine not having him to talk to and to do things with. I felt scared when I tried to imagine life without Dad. How would he have handled a situation like this? He probably would have chopped some wood. He would have kept busy.

These feelings took me back to when I was a child, back to when Dad's mother passed away. I remembered the dread I had felt back then. I remembered telling myself, "It must be horrible not to have a mother anymore." Through the years, when that memory would come to mind, I wondered what I would do when the time came for me to deal with the death of one of my parents. The time had come, and I didn't want to deal with it. But I had to find a way to come to terms with this terrible and horrifying loss. Keeping busy would help, but I didn't believe it would ultimately be the best and only way to handle things. It would just delay the real work to be done.

Without realizing it, I had begun this process before leaving Oregon for Dad's funeral. I called friends and told them what happened. I called my husband's parents and shared my grief and shock with them. I left a note for the man and woman I call my "surrogate parents," who were out of town. I needed people to know what happened. I called my brother and talked to him. Later I would call Mom; she wouldn't be someone to help me. She would look to me for support, and I wasn't up to that right now. We packed our things and headed out. Now, at his home, I found myself trying to hold on to Dad by looking at his household belongings. I remembered his hands, strong and worn from work, hands that had taught me many things. I didn't even try to hold back the tears. There was no need.

I slowly opened the door to Dad's room. I had no idea of what I would see. David told me that he and a friend had cleaned it. David apologized and warned, "It isn't spotless but it's a lot better than it was." I was thankful that they did the cleaning. Most everything had to be thrown out and the room repainted. I couldn't imagine how they were able to do it. The room was almost bare. The stark light shone in through bare windows. Sounds echoed in the room. I stood at the door and found myself trying to imagine Dad's last moments. Was he crying? Was he calm? Did he take his life because he felt there was no other choice? Was he thinking of me? Was he thinking of my little boys and how they would feel without their grandpa? Did he know I loved him? Did he know how much it meant to me to call him Dad? What about all of the "unfinished business?" Was he angry? Did he know how empty life would be without him, without Dad? Why did he hurry death?

These questions came weaving in and out as I stood in his

room. One question led to others, and all of them had no answers. Here I stood in horror, trying to weave a pattern of sense, only to be interrupted by the image of the gun blast, the image of Dad kneeling beside the bed and pulling the trigger. I opened the closet doors and felt the sleeves of the shirts he wore. With all the cleaning that had been done, there was still more to be done. Having a glimpse of what happened in this room helped me to know it was real. It was horrifying, and it was real. I was glad the room was not sterile. I needed to experience for myself the horror, and yet I was deeply thankful I did not see what David saw. I was deeply thankful for the thought and care given by David's friend when he helped with cleaning up the room.

The funeral would be the next day. We spent the night in Grandpa's house. The boys wanted to be there, and they had started to realize they would not see Grandpa again. They would forget being told he died and would ask, "When is Grandpa going to get here?" I didn't know if we would ever come to this place again either, so I too wanted to stay here. I was surprised to find I slept soundly for a few hours. I had at first worried about what people would think of me staying in Dad's house after what happened, but I decided to listen to what my heart was telling me. Let people think their thoughts. Many times before I had acted to please others and regretted it. Listening to my heart turned out to be the best choice I could have made for where to spend the night and for what to do in the future.

Early the next morning Dad's brother knocked on the door. He, too, had come from out of town. We talked for a few minutes about what would happen that day. I noticed that he was looking around, and I told him he was free to walk around. When he, too, needed to see Dad's room I realized there are things we do when we are grieving that we ordinarily wouldn't do. Grief has a sense of its own. A huge weight had been lifted—I wasn't "losing my mind."

The few hours before the funeral were hectic. We got to the funeral home early so I could take some pictures. The boys were young, and I wanted to have something for the future when they have questions. I was not sure where to sit, somewhere up front. Many family members have had their funerals here. I sat and remembered those people as friends came in. The service began. The minister stood at the podium. We had never met. He was talking to a group of simple, rural people. He was talking to a group who had attended church for weddings and funerals but seldom for other reasons. As he talked, I realized he was not connecting with the people in the pews. They did not know the point of what he was saying. I was deeply hurt and angered. To others he sounded as if he was speaking nonsense. To me, I knew he was using this gathering to "save lost souls" and not to offer hope or comfort. Not once did he mention Dad's name, that he was a father, a grandfather, a brother, an uncle, a friend. I was outraged! We came to grieve the loss of a loved one, and yet he was not given a name or relationship! Instead we heard, "And for you older ones, you might be wondering if this could've been you." I was outraged! This was not just some dead man in a casket—it was my father, my sons' grandfather! Everyone there had been deeply affected by this man's death, and yet from the minister there were no words that offered comfort or understanding.

Later, while friends and other family members waited for us outside, my siblings and our families said our final goodbyes to our father. It was a painful, awkward moment. I wanted words of encouragement, words of understanding. The minister stood to the side and watched us. I was again angry and offended by his lack of compassion and support.

My oldest son, who was seven years old, was sad and quiet. He said he would miss Grandpa, and he didn't know why he killed himself. At this moment I wished he hadn't overheard the phone call. No words I could say would make sense of it all. I didn't understand why myself. My youngest son, who was five years old, was angry. He said he would not say goodbye. I touched the closed casket and asked the boys if they wanted to. They said no. I said, "Thank you, Dad, for everything. I love you, and I miss you." I wished I could see him one last time. I wished I could touch him one last time.

After a brief graveside service my husband, Edgars, myself, and the boys stayed on to watch the workers complete the burial from a hillside across the way. The boys wanted to watch. They asked questions about burying people. What is the inside of a coffin like? Do people have their clothes on? Why do people have to be buried? These questions are answerable ones. It was a relief to have answers for a change. I told my sons that I didn't know why Grandpa ended his life. I told them I would let them know why when I figured it out. They seemed relieved. They were more upbeat and talkative, ready to play again. Believing an answer would come seemed to be enough for the boys for now.

We spent some time looking at the headstones of the relatives I remembered. I showed them where my grandparents were buried. I shared my memories with them. I didn't know what they were thinking. They tried their best to put their feelings and thoughts to words. Words seemed such inadequate clothing for feelings at the time. I could see how limited they were in expressing this experience with words. They were frustrated when they tried to explain something and I just couldn't "get it right."

Later I bought some paper and crayons for them to draw on. Since they couldn't express what they wanted to with words maybe they could with pictures. This was a valuable insight. Through their pictures I became more aware of their thoughts and feelings. I started to learn what questions to ask them to help them with their experience, questions about their pictures. I noted that neither boy had cried very much, but in their pictures they drew themselves crying lots of tears. While talking together the tears would come, little by little. I let them see me cry, and I told them why when they asked. I also shared happy memories. It was important to keep a balance to the memories. It was so easy to be sad.

For the next few days my siblings and our families were together. At times tears would come. No one asked for explanations, and no one tried to stop the tears. They were simply allowed to be. This was a new thing for our family, and it felt good. We went over Dad's will. We sat in his house and talked. We even laughed a little at some memories. We decided to go to the airport in Dad's truck, just like old times. Dust was flying up, and we were ducking branches. We laughed and enjoyed reliving the past.

Before leaving for Oregon, I went to the cemetery and "talked" with Dad. Earlier that morning I had gone to Dad's place and walked around. I listened to the sounds of birds and crickets and to the hum of an airplane high overhead. I felt the bark of trees. I went to the old cabin where we lived before the house was built. I drank from the old spring. I turned on the hose and watered the ground. It smelled like it does when it rains. It was a comforting smell. I went to the garden and put some soil in a container to take with me. It was soil that Dad and I had worked together for the gardens we had planted.

Then it was time to go. It was hard to leave. I didn't want to leave this well-known place. The trees were the same; the spring, the sky, the mountains were the same, but now they were also different because Dad was gone. Dad had made this place special. And yet, in a smaller way it remained special because he had taught me to love this place. Such mixed emotions.

Once on the road, we drove in silence for a long time. Everything I saw held memories. With every memory came the reminder that Dad had died, and right after that came the memory of how. What I saw in his room came flashing back again and again. I tried to stop this cycle, but I couldn't.

We stopped in central Oregon to see Edgars's folks on our way home. They didn't ask a lot of questions. They let me talk when I felt I could. There was no right or wrong way for me to be. I could just be me. A friend called me at their house to see how I was. It felt so wonderful to have someone reach out to me. I couldn't reach out. I wanted to tell others that I needed them to reach out to me but I couldn't. The words wouldn't come. I couldn't keep the days straight or remember things. I was extremely forgetful. Without realizing it, I was beginning the downward spiral of depression.

When we arrived home, I found myself keeping busier than usual. We were packing to move to Detroit, where my husband had just received a call to a new congregation. This move meant leaving family and friends, but I told myself I could handle it. Suddenly close friends became more distant and were not home when I called. I felt abandoned by those I had believed would be there for me. This became one of many turning points in my life. I decided not to run after these now-distant friends. I was in a struggle for my own life, to still parent my children, to still be a wife, to understand who I was in light of Dad's suicide.

Every day it seemed I had more questions than answers. Beliefs about life, about the church, and about friendships no longer had the simple defining framework they had had just a few weeks before. I questioned everything I felt, every perception and conviction I had. So much of the world had been defined by Dad. Did my convictions still hold true or did his suicide change the truth of things?

A pivotal question concerned Dad's teachings about persevering through life's difficulties. Did those teachings still hold true? Dad had been a Rock of Gibraltar for me. It seemed that no matter how incredibly difficult life was at times, he managed to keep going. I had to ask, "Now what?" Was Dad serious about dealing with life's difficulties all those years, or was he just trying to make things sound good? Did he really believe the things he was telling me? If he did believe them, then why suicide? If he didn't believe what he told me, then should I? Why persevere if we give up at some point anyway? Another thought came to mind, one that was very painful to consider at the time and that is still painful today. Could it be that Dad's decision didn't have anything to do with believing or not believing what he taught? Could it be that Dad, this icon of strength, simply found himself in a situation where his perseverance ran out? Could I "allow" Dad not to be strong all the time? Does my sense of well-being depend on Dad overcoming hardships in his own life? Was he, rather than running from a hard decision, indeed facing it? Could it be that for Dad, suicide was not a way out, but one difficult choice taken from a list of difficult choices? Could it be his thoughts had nothing to do with strength or weakness? I couldn't check with Dad on this one. I was on my own. Earlier I could always call and ask Dad a question, but there was no more calling. I still dialed his number and listened to the phone ring. I pictured it ringing on the wall, and I could almost hear him say, "Hello." There was no more "running it by Dad" anymore. I had to search within myself for answers, and I didn't trust myself.

I wanted to believe there was meaning to life. I wanted to believe this meaning was significant and worth persevering. I didn't want to believe it was okay to end life when difficulties came. I wanted there to be a solution, an alternative. Having my own children reminded me of how precious life is. My Christian faith gave me the conviction that life was a gift, a gift to be cherished. This task at hand of coming to terms with Dad's suicide wasn't just for me, it was for my children as well. Somehow I had to get through this crisis.

The questions I asked of myself changed from "should I?" or "could I?" to "how do I?" By my questioning and talking I realized some truths for me. One truth for me is that conversation is not a waste of time! Without the gift of conversation I wouldn't have been able to begin the work of coming to terms with Dad's death. Conversation doesn't get the wood cut, but it comes in handy with other things. Eventually I was able to say, "Dad, it is okay not to be strong all the time. It's okay you couldn't overcome this one . . . . I am okay. You are gone but I am okay. I have things to work on but I will get through this." I began to live my separateness from Dad in ways new to me. Perhaps this is what all of us strive to do when we "leave home."

I didn't hear the words I wanted so much to hear at Dad's funeral, and this was weighing on me. I shared this hurt and need with my "surrogate parents" (a college professor and his wife). They listened as I poured out my grief and anger. They listened and acknowledged my pain and confusion. There were no corrections of what I said, no efforts to minimize the horror I felt, no advice to "keep a stiff upper lip." We sat at the tea table and spoke of these things. I felt anchored by their ability to listen and care. Through those conversations came the words I needed to hear: words of comfort and understanding, words from Scripture that reminded me of God's loving presence as Dad struggled with the decision he made. I needed to hear that just as Dad was not alone, I am not alone. The very thing the minister had tried to "prove" by quoting Scripture, I now experienced. My pain and questions were not hurried away. In being reminded, in knowing that I wasn't alone came the first step in the process of healing and putting my life back together.

IV

After our move across the country, after a few months of living in Detroit, more of life crumbled as my husband and I both tried to cope with depression. We felt isolated and cut off. Our move proved more difficult than I had expected. Edgars's new call had many things to work out, and I needed Edgars to do many of the things I used to do. Things did not look good. I was not eating or sleeping. I was irritable, tired, and just plain miserable to live with. My health was suffering. I worried about the impact on the kids, on all of us. I struggled to keep going. I volunteered at the boys' school just to have something to get up for. I felt guilty about struggling like this. It was hard to be there for the little things my kids were doing and learning, let alone the bigger things. I had worked so hard to be the best parent I could be, and now I felt utterly derailed.

No one wanted to hear about Dad, or they said things that made it worse. I gave up trying to find someone to talk with locally. Our phone bill was monstrous because I called the West Coast so often. I felt guilty about that, but I had to talk with someone. I felt like I was going crazy. I wrote in my journal and wrote poems. It helped a great deal. Sometimes it was difficult to pick up the phone. All I could think of is that I couldn't call home anymore. I would still dial the phone number when I couldn't sleep sometimes. I would listen to it ring and ring until the operator came on the line. Eventually the phone was disconnected. I felt disconnected.

I could no longer stand to do the grocery shopping. Too many memories of Dad. Passing the meat department proved too much for me, and I feared I would have a nervous breakdown in the store. Reminders of Dad's room. So Edgars did the shopping. He hadn't said too much about Dad's death or anything. I appreciated all of his help. I appreciated him not expecting me to help him grieve Dad's death. I worried about Edgars though. He needed to find someone with whom to cry. I couldn't help him mourn and he couldn't help me. It sounds bad but that is how it was.

In many ways we drifted apart. Who knows what the future holds. He needed to get back on his feet. He was deeply depressed. I wanted him to be strong again. To feel good again. I was afraid to say anything. I was extremely angry and resentful of him being so depressed. "After all," I said to myself, "it was my father, not his!" I told myself, "Wanda, that isn't the way it works!" but saying that didn't help. I felt let down and that I needed to be strong when I didn't think I could be. I didn't want to be strong. I wanted to be sad. I wanted to say that I miss my dad. I wanted to say so many things to him. I wanted to tell him about our move, the weather, the beautiful birds, our new home, and how the boys are doing. When I think of being sixty years old and not having a dad, I cry. I'll always want my dad. We didn't have enough time together.

As a result of Dad's suicide, I panic easily. I'm afraid some horrible thing will happen suddenly, unexpectedly. I could not have imagined something hurting so profoundly as Dad's death. Now I know and I am afraid. I'm afraid this kind of pain will come again somewhere, somehow. Following Dad's death, there were days I couldn't leave the house. I couldn't even walk in the neighborhood. Even Edgars was unsuccessful at getting me to go places with him. I knew I was in trouble. I had isolated myself more and more. Edgars called around to inquire about bereavement groups. Everyone told him I needed a group that dealt specifically with suicide. No one had any references. I was able to stay calm, but I felt anger toward Dad. Edgars tried his best to help but I rejected him. I was angry at the world.

When the boys became upset or frustrated they would say, "I feel like killing myself." Our youngest son, who is named after his grandfather, said he wanted to change his name because of "what Grandpa did." He said, "It's hard to explain. What Grandpa did makes me feel bad about myself, especially when I think about our names." Now how does a person deal with this? I read books and called counselors, and no one knew what to tell me. The response was, "That's a new one. I've never had someone say that to me." I ventured maybe my son could change his name. Some people didn't like the idea of a name change.

We talked about it, and I could see that my son needed a reprieve from the situation he was in. I asked questions and more questions, trying to understand what he was thinking and feeling. When I asked him what he would like to do to solve this problem, he said unequivocally, "I want to change my name." My thought was, "Great! This kid has an idea of something to try." So we talked about names for a few weeks as he considered different ones. Finally he settled on the first name of my "surrogate dad" and the boys' surrogate granddad. My son holds this man in high esteem, and so he chose his name. I am hoping this is a psychologically sound choice. With time, I have found that my children are working through their loss on two levels—the loss of the person who has completed suicide, and how this affects their parent.

About seven months after Dad's death, a flyer came to the church regarding a suicide survivor support group. I decided to call; it seemed like it would be helpful. Edgars drove me to the meeting place. I wouldn't have gotten there if I had to drive myself, because I would have panicked. I went in and sat down. I was amazed at how many other people were in the room. The leaders outlined the purpose of the group, and then we took turns going around the circle explaining who we lost to suicide. We shared tears over the mothers, fathers, brothers, sisters, grandchildren, and friends we had lost to suicide. It was one of the most difficult times in my life. These people could relate to my pain, and yet it was so hard to share it. I didn't want to hear any more platitudes or insensitive comments. I was tired of dealing with people's well-intentioned but ignorant statements.

In the weeks that followed we shared our anguish and the thoughts and behaviors we had once thought odd. I came to see that I was normal. We are incredibly resourceful at surviving and comforting ourselves. While our behavior, under different circumstances, might legitimately be cause for concern, the behaviors we have resorted to since losing a loved one to suicide made perfect sense. What a relief to hear others acting like me—acknowledging how hard it was to come to the group, panicking, not eating, not sleeping, running the suicide over and over in the their heads, wondering if they could have prevented it, wondering if there was something they had overlooked.

The survivors' group is the place I come to be with Dad again. This is where I come to make sense of the world again. This is where I come to mourn in a safe place. This is where I come when I don't want to be alone with my loss. The suicide survivors' group has been crucial to rebuilding my life. Through the leadership of the group I was able to connect with a therapist and get the professional help I need. I learned that there are places and people with whom I can share my experience. I am slowly regaining my sense of well-being and strength. It feels wonderful!

I keep mementos of Dad in meaningful places. I keep his picture on the wall, and I speak of him almost daily. I use what he taught me, and in that way spend time with him. In the passing of almost six years' time I have overcome many obstacles. I would not want to experience a suicide death again, but neither would I want to give up what I have learned about myself. Life has become more meaningful and purposeful. I have a new sense of what is ultimately important to me. My siblings and I have tried to piece things together over the months. It has helped to talk. We have talked more in the last few months than we have in years. We've taken care of some old secrets. Some good things are happening. Friendships that have weathered the last four years have become richer and more meaningful. Some friendships have fallen by the wayside, I am okay with that.

Forming new friendships has become a challenge for me. It is difficult for me to become attached to others. I have to work at it in a way I didn't before. I enjoy the company of others, but I do not seek to know them as I once did. I protect myself from getting close to new friends and losing them, from fear of hurting so deeply again.

While I don't like this about myself, it is enough for now to have some moments together and to go our separate ways. Someday I hope things are different. I work on resolving this little by little. I see that as I come to terms with Dad's suicide I am able to connect a bit more intimately with others. I strive to give myself the gift of tomorrow. I remind myself that not everything needs to be taken care of today. I reassure myself that I can live with the pain and loss of my dad. And in doing this I can live with the pain of losing others.

As I continue to come to terms with my loss, I teach my children that they too can come to terms with life-changing loss. They watch and learn how to mourn, how to question, how to make sense of things. They learn that life goes on. They learn that they are okay. Together, we've had wonderful talks about Grandpa. Talking about Grandpa keeps him with us in meaningful ways. Each year we buy Grandpa's favorite flowers and plant them in our yard. This year I might plant red petunias, which were Dad's favorite. On birthdays and holidays the boys get a gift "from Grandpa"; they understand it is from me for the memory of Grandpa. We've drawn pictures of the suicide, of the funeral, of Grandpa in heaven, of why we think Grandpa took his life. We've drawn pictures of ourselves at the beach with Grandpa and of Grandpa with his dog. Pictures helped when we couldn't find the words. The pictures have changed as the boys have grown. As they understand more they add to their pictures. My children's pictures have helped me to know what they understood and what they could accept. It was okay to be angry at Grandpa, okay to miss him, and okay to love him even though he died. The boys seldom say, "I feel like killing myself," anymore. My youngest son is considering using his original name again, although he is very fond of his new one. With this change, I sense he has come to terms with some troubles of his own. As he continues to work through his many questions and thoughts, I see that allowing him to change his name has helped tremendously. It was not so much the actual changing of names that has been helpful, but being supported in trying to grapple with his experience based on his own ideas.

I still have concerns about the boys in the future. We have had many conversations about what to do when we are feeling depressed, sad and angry. I am sure we will have many more. We do not joke about suicide or killing ourselves, and we do not play with toy guns. I am glad the boys can openly talk about Grandpa killing himself when the topic comes up or when they need to. It has taken people by surprise. In their own way they are breaking the code of silence about suicide. While it is not their favorite thing to talk about, they are able to share their thoughts and feelings about it.

There are those who question telling young children about a suicide. In my case, the children overheard the phone call. But even if they hadn't overheard it, I would have told them. They would have asked, "How?" I don't think I would have handled things any differently than I did. That is not to say I told them every detail. I told them, "Grandpa died. He shot himself. Grandpa was depressed, and he was beginning to imagine things. This was very scary for him. He was afraid someone was going to take him away from his home. He didn't want anyone to have to take care of him, and he didn't want to leave his home. He thought ending his life was the best thing to do." We talk about how heartbreaking it was for us that Grandpa took his life. We talk about how it was a choice he made and that there were other choices he could have made. We talk about how it was no one's fault that Grandpa took his life. Whenever the boys show an interest in talking about these things, we do. I don't push it. The questions and the talks come and go with no set rhythm.

As for me, I continue to sift through my childhood, to sift through Dad's life and death. I still try to make sense of Dad's suicide. I see that I am separate from my dad. I know that what was true for Dad is not necessarily true for me. My life and circumstances are different, and that is okay. I am no longer depressed. I can sleep and eat. I can do the grocery shopping. I continue to talk about Dad. Once in a while I uncover something new in the wisdom he had, and I am grateful for it. My sons are doing well, and they continue to add new understanding to their experiences as they grow. Edgars and I continue to grieve independently. We have realized, in large part from Dad's suicide, that we sometimes need a place apart from each other to live our lives and grieve, whether this means to go for walks alone or to spend time with other people. It is okay not to be all things to each other. In writing this essay Edgars and I were able to share more of our personal grief and that has been very helpful to both of us. I am surviving and so is my family. We have managed to remain a family, and we are working on becoming strong.

In 1997, Edgars's brother committed suicide. Though the loss has been painful, we have been able to face each day with the confidence of knowing we will survive this loss as well. We have learned many valuable ways in which to recover from loss such as this. We have learned it takes determination to make life enjoyable again.

Writing poetry has helped me to express my feelings, thoughts, and experiences. I am including three of my poems that have special meaning to me.

Visitors

> It feels like the memories get lonely
> so they knock until I stay up with them.
> I try to put them out of mind
> but they flicker like a stubborn candle.
> I find myself wandering the places I'd rather not go,
> places which too many of us have been

but none of us ever wanted to be.
Unsatiable memories carry me away,
I, unaware of their mesmerizing hold
walk through the darkened halls and
sneak peeks of things in forbidden rooms.
The reasons for my reluctance to come look back at me
and I jump back out of view, my heart pounding.
It is only now that I know I answered their knock.
Oddly though, the memories have taken their leave
but I know they'll be back, when they get lonely.

Shackles Once Removed

Bent shelves are holding dormant feelings fast.
A few were intentionally placed upon the shelves
While others unconsciously found there a post at last.
Bits of dust danced about as if tiny elves
When with a finger's brushing I disturbed their rest.
As I considered my setting those feelings free
Images wishful of expression mimed a quest
Ended only by my setting those feelings free.

The Given Name

Feelings without identity stroke my consciousness
As they contradict and play with each other.
They silently, persistently tease with finesse.
The restlessness within begins to wither
When by chance a feeling is given a name.
Surprising calm and time to breathe deep, letting go.
New consciousness ebbs and flows, something beyond shame.
Compelled, I struggle to comfort the confusion I know.
I'm on my way, feelings with names and faces,
Though many still paired in conflict.

They've become more like friends who share embraces.

Feelings in kaleidoscopic form, an edict

Not so intimidating, not so distorted.

Wanda Ford-Petrevics

Wanda Ford-Petrevics was thirty-two in 1996 when
her father, aged eighty-one, completed suicide.

A Saving Curse

My father killed himself in the January of my second year in college. I was nineteen years old. His suicide did not come as a total surprise to me. I had anticipated it during the years leading up to my parents' separation; he was so vulnerable. During high school, I had done a lot of writing about suicide, but that was as far as I dared express my concern about my father. Unfortunately, no one ever picked up on it, and I never could get myself to talk to anyone about it. The "plus" side of my awareness was that his suicide was not the shock to me that it was to my siblings. But the price I paid for this was high. For years, I was burdened by an inflated sense of responsibility and guilt. I had known he was in trouble, and yet I had said nothing. Even worse, I feared my thoughts had made it happen. Although nearly an adult, I maintained a child's magical thinking—that my worries and fears had made it happen.

At the time of my father's death in 1972, there was no Suicide Prevention Center to go to for support (if it even had occurred to me that I needed support). When my mother called me at college to tell me that my dad was dead, I left school, went home for a memorial service, and was back at school three days later. I don't remember any conversations with my sisters, my brother, or my mother about Dad's suicide. And certainly once I was back at college, I never talked to anyone about my father's death. I came back to my Dante class in time for the lecture on the circle in hell that included all the suicides, their souls hanging from trees. That pretty much put a stop to any inclination I might have had to share this event with anyone. Unfortunately, it was eighteen years before I got any help.

I made three immediate conclusions upon my father's death:

1. He didn't love me enough to stay alive for me.

With his marriage over, somehow we four children were not enough for my dad to live for. It was hard then to believe that my father loved us, loved me. I spent about ten years filled with anger against my father for taking his life. Underneath the anger was the painful conviction that I had not been important to my own parent. I decided that I had been mistaken in thinking he had ever loved me; he had just loved my support and that I didn't give him any trouble. He didn't really love me. Lurking even deeper was the devastating thought that it was actually my fault he didn't love me—I wasn't lovable. I wasn't worth anything. I wasn't worth living for. It is hard to even begin to explain the impact this corrosive doubt had in my life. I have a history of accepting inappropriate behavior and mistreatment from others. The concept of "I don't deserve this" did not enter my head for over twenty years. Instead, I believed I did deserve bad treatment from others, not for any reason in the present, but for my "sin" of not getting help for my father. My dad was right not to consider me. There was something wrong with me. I was a bad person. I deserved to be punished.

Eighteen years later, when I finally got into a LOSS (Loving Outreach for Survivors of Suicide) group at my local Suicide Prevention and Crisis Center, I learned that someone who is deeply depressed cannot think of anything or anyone else. The pain is everything. Later, I learned from my mother that my father's father had gone through a period of depression at the same "midlife crisis" age as my dad. He, too, had been suicidal. He was treated with electric shock therapy. So I began to wonder, when my father got far enough into his depression that he was unable to think clearly, had the image of his own father's ordeal played a part in his suicide? Perhaps he was afraid that he, too, would be forced to submit to this frightening procedure that had left his own father much changed. And maybe there was shame here, too. Suicide became a way to avoid both a feared treatment and the associated shame. While this helped to answer my "How could he do this to us if he loved us?" question, it opened up a new can of worms—I have two generations of family members (that I know of) who have had breakdowns and have either thought of or completed suicide. Will my brother, my two sisters, and I get through our late forties? And, if we do, will we even then be "safe"?

2. I will never do this to my children.

When I realized at age thirty-eight that I wanted to be dead, it scared me so much that I finally accepted that I would have to get out of my marriage. Up until then I had been kept in the marriage by the idea that a pattern was in operation—if I left my husband, he would commit suicide as my father had done when he and my mother split up. I had associated divorce and suicide in my mind ever since I was nineteen. Then suddenly, the one in danger was me, not my husband. It was only when I realized this that I got the courage to leave. I believe I have already been saved by the resolution I made in regard to my own children. Therefore, I have some grounds for trusting it to get me through the rest of my life.

3. I am responsible for the lives of others.

I was living with my boyfriend at college at the time of my dad's death. My father made it clear that he was very disappointed in me. His disapproval was very hard for me—I had always been "Miss Perfect Daughter." I didn't like my boyfriend very much (I was just, unfortunately, in love with him), but two years later we got married. Neither one of us really wanted to. We're not together now, so I can't say what motivated my boyfriend, but I know how I felt about it. I felt that I had to marry him to prove to my father I was a respectable person. Then I spent the next sixteen years trying to prove myself to my husband. I never succeeded. I wish I had realized I needed to prove myself only to myself, but I didn't. That old lack of self-worth kept me continually trying harder and harder "to please." It was not a good marriage. I'm sorry I wasted so much of my life stubbornly determined to make it work because in my adolescent audacity, I had imagined my parents had not tried hard enough. It was very scary for me to get a divorce. I felt my husband was weaker and more dependent than my father had been, so if my father had not survived, how could my husband? I realize now that I had an exaggerated belief in my own power and importance.

When I went off to college, I felt very guilty for leaving my dad. Several times during my last summer at home (during which I worked with him at his office), he would say he didn't know what he was going to do without me. I would hear him say things like "Who am I going to watch movies with when you're gone? Who am I going to talk about work things with?" I'm sure my dad was trying to say he was going to miss me, and that is nice for a child to know, but it went beyond that. I felt worried. I felt responsible for him. I was the one in the family who supported him emotionally, and I felt as though I were abandoning him. Seven months after I left, my parents split up. Eight months after that, my dad killed himself. There. You see—he couldn't survive without me. I left him; he died. Cause, effect.

Twenty years later, I expected the same consequence in my own divorce. The man I married would fall apart without me. I just could not go through another suicide. I could not be responsible for another suicide. I was trapped. Going to the LOSS group was the first step in ending my marriage. I knew if I could stop feeling responsible for my father, I could stop feeling responsible for my husband. It was a hard road. Grieving after eighteen years is difficult to do. I had no contact with my feelings. I had to listen to other people to slowly regain and verbalize my own suppressed feelings. Just listening to all these people who had lost someone and who had been unable to prevent the tragedy helped me. I was not responsible for my father's life or death. I was the child in the situation. I gradually let go of the conviction that I was responsible for my father's death. And as a consequence, I also stopped thinking that I was responsible for my husband's life. I was finally able to put an end to my "punishment."

Sometime last year I wrote down a sentence that repeated in my head. I think it is the first sentence in the story of my life. It goes like this: *My father's suicide cursed me; it also saved my life.* I am fully aware of the damage my father's suicide did to me. I regret that I did not get professional help for so many years because, if I had, I know that the damage would have been so much less. My father's suicide dominated my life for twenty-five years. But I am convinced that my dad's death has given me certain strengths. Among them is a strong grasp on the responsibility I have—the responsibility to live. Recognizing my suicidal feelings once rescued me from a bad situation. Since then, there have been times when I have deeply resented my father for taking away from me the option of suicide. Sometimes when I crash emotionally, the feeling of failure is overwhelming, and the idea of not having to deal with pain is attractive. But the road of suicide is not open to me. Knowing the effect it has on survivors, I could never do that to those I love. I would never forgive myself, and I know, only too well, they might never forgive me. That is a frightening and sobering thought. So I can honestly say that my father's death has kept and continues to keep me alive. And that is how he saves me. He has made the choice clear for me. I must ride out my pain so that I don't give others unending pain. With some sorrow, I must confess that there can be value in a negative model.

Suzanne Gardner

Suzanne Gardner was nineteen in 1972 when her
father, aged forty-seven, completed suicide.

I Will Not Die of Regret:
A Letter to My Father

The last time I saw you was in Newark Airport. I was flying back to the West Coast after visiting with you alone for several days. I had hoped we could talk more personally this time, but you deflected my questions with the usual short answers. It made me sad, but I didn't press you. You walked me to the entrance of the gates, and we hugged. I turned back once to wave and saw you standing, watching me, practically a silhouette, with huge bright windows behind you and cars flitting beyond. The crowds of travelers eddied and swirled around you, and you looked out of place, suddenly small. I wanted to run back and make everything slow down. The world was moving too fast for you now. I saw it in how you stood there, like a man over his waist in a river, uncertain where to step next. I wonder if you felt it too. In that instant I knew you would never see me off at the airport again. I waved heavily, my arm pushing against water, and turned to the gates, dizzy and choked by this huge certainty. Maybe you were already leaving the world then, before my eyes. This was the summer before you died.

It's like a blow to my own body. Ten years later, in my monthly grief group, I am still shocked to hear myself say, "My father killed himself on December 1, 1986."

You used a shotgun to your head in your home office at 4:00 A.M. while Mom was sleeping. She said your face was intact; the shot tore off the back of the head. She sat on the soaked rug with you until the ambulance came, saying goodbye. I don't know if I believe what she says about your face. Why does that even matter? The damage was much more widespread anyway.

Dad, I'm writing this to you. I've never spoken to you like this, alive or dead, and, finally, ten years later, I feel that I can. You know how I miss you, though I don't miss the pain you carried with you. It is a relief not to see you weighed down like that.

My life has re-formed around the wound of your death like a tree growing over barbed wire. I have changed. Now I am grateful for this, though I would never thank you for what you did. I can truly say that my life began when you died.

What drove you to kill yourself? You were sober in the years before you died, after struggling with depression and alcohol for decades. Were you afraid of being helpless in your old age? Maybe you woke up at age sixty-nine and saw your life had not turned out as you thought it should. You had wanted to be a teacher, a book author, a "man of distinction" like famous figures in the biographies you devoured. No matter that you'd had a successful business career. Did you stay in it out of duty to us? Now it was too late. The regret was killing you, so you just finished the job. I don't need to know anymore why you killed yourself. There isn't any one answer, either. Only that your life was unendurable, and you never spoke of it. But these questions consumed me at the beginning.

Your death woke me up, Dad. I was thirty-three. I had just begun graduate school in a master of fine arts program, arriving after a circuitous journey following college. I was embarking on my life as an artist. I wanted to see if this was who I really was, did I have what it takes? I was carving out time in my life in order to find out. I felt that I was worth it, but I was scared. I had limited experience in taking risks. You thought I was crazy to give up a good job to go back to school.

I am so grateful that I had art and the structure of school to help me make sense of this unthinkable thing that exploded in my life. My teachers encouraged me to explore my grief through art. I made masks, drawings, and photographs; wrote journals and performance pieces; and created a movement elegy to acknowledge your life.

Your death made me see that, even then, I wasn't fully seizing my life, not deeply, fiercely, from within. Your death waved a warning: This could happen to me if I didn't act on my true desires right now, at every moment. There was no time to postpone anything, no time to waste. I swore then, "I will not die of regret."

Photography, my major in school and a passion for the past seven years, suddenly lost meaning for me. I had been working on a series of black-and-white photographs of myself nude, using double exposures and slow shutter speeds to blur movement. They were very sensual, and I was pleased with them. Yet when I looked at these images after you died there was nothing familiar about them. I couldn't connect those pictures to me. I heard a voice in my head ask, "Who made these? Who is that person in the photos? What does she have to do with me?" I had no desire to finish the series.

I realized that I could no longer celebrate life from behind the lens of a camera. Photography was a way of bringing the world closer without having to touch it or be in the thick of it. It was essentially a solitary observer's art, an art of longing, stuck at the fringes, an art of regret. I now needed to speak out in person, directly, with nothing in my way. I wanted to create art in the presence of other people, to share my body and voice, fully alive. Your death tore down the barriers inside me and forced me to step forward. I had no choice.

Delivering the eulogy at your memorial service was that first step into a new medium—theater—a collaborative, living art that feels like home. My delight in writing plays and in performing had first blossomed in grammar school, but somehow I lost sight of this; I don't even know how or when. I will always be grateful that your death compelled me to reexcavate my true desires.

Mom told me you had died. I knew immediately that I had to

speak at the memorial. I needed something beyond the existing ritual and knew that I had the power to create it myself. I stood before a church overflowing with people and felt that something had dropped cleanly into place in my life. I had taken action. I could hardly keep up with the sound of my voice as I read what I had written. It was a tribute to you in the form of a walk around our property, up the lane, around the woodpile and the garden, ending at the towering Dawn Redwood tree you had planted as a seedling, the tree that will outlive all of us. Speaking flowed out of me, ordering the disarray of your death, praising your life. Afterwards many people thanked me for saying what they hadn't known they were feeling. I realized that in acting on my own need to speak, I had spoken for all of us. I could hardly absorb what this meant, but I knew I had done something very powerful. It showed me that my instincts were right, and I kept on following them. Now as a teacher, I try to reflect for others the wisdom of their own instincts. I think maybe you weren't able to hear the voice of your own instincts.

In school, I redesigned my major to include off-campus courses in theater, improvisation, and creative movement. From these choices other opportunities unfolded: I received a year-long residency with a stipend at an experimental arts center. In my interview, I spoke to a responsive panel about how your death had strengthened my commitment as an artist at the same time that it propelled me in a new direction. The next year I was accepted in an apprenticeship program for teaching theater and movement in elementary and middle schools, and I felt I had found my niche. This is the work I continue today, with a sense of fulfillment that is stronger each year. I am always energized by calling forth the creativity of young people.

In these ten years I have come to understand more and more the meaning of your death. I listen to the people in my grief group; we are all filled with questions. We realize that the ones who died are mystery people—to us, to themselves. We are left with the despair that we never really knew you. How could we? You wouldn't let us. Your deaths tear into these mysteries, throwing gashes of light into ancient sealed tombs, like King Tut's, which so fascinated you. I have had to accept that there will always be a mystery about you.

Nowadays I prefer the company of people who are also questioning. Why am I alive? Why am I left behind? This time is given to me to make sense of the loss. I want to use it well. Your death opened up my depths, and I am impatient with superficiality now. It wastes my time.

Mom also wonders why she is left behind. At seventy-seven she still needs time to heal the loss of you. She does not often allow herself to cry. Her grieving is knotted with guilt; she believes she could have done something to help you. I see that my healing in these ten years has made me ready, finally, to listen to her without judging or trying to solve her pain.

The first years after you died were so hard. All of us became exaggerated versions of ourselves. Mom maintained a stoic front since this was "what your father would have wanted." I was the oldest sister, expected to be strong and take charge. The siblings withdrew into their own lives. At first I could not accept that each of us chose to cope in our own way. I longed for closeness from the family, but I only drove them farther away by my emotional rawness and desire to talk. This tragedy did not bring us closer together. I felt totally alone.

The local paper did not print the cause of your death. I don't know how this was arranged, but I'm sure you would have approved. Mom made it clear to us that this information was private, except among the closest friends and family. Of course I didn't agree. It made me furious. It was one more instance in a lifetime of being trained to bury difficult feelings and put up the "happy family" front. Your suicide completely destroyed any semblance of those good appearances, and we still had to keep on pretending? It was exhausting, and I was fed up with it. Four years later, when I spoke about you on a national television program on elder suicide, local people called Mom to express their shock and surprise at learning how you died. I was naive, to say the least, about the consequences of speaking out. I know I caused Mom much pain, and I am sorry. I would handle the situation very differently today.

This incident caused a huge rift in our relationship. We argued over the ethics of "telling the truth," and I saw for the first time in my life how thoroughly and absolutely we disagreed on this issue. I felt condemned and negated for the principles I live by. Coming from my own mother this opinion was devastating. I imagine Mom must have felt much the same way. We didn't speak to each other for over a year. During that time I had a deep gaping sensation in my body whenever I thought of her. It felt like she had died, too; she was gone completely. I didn't expect to talk to her ever again.

I don't regret speaking out, but I wish I had been more savvy about talking to the media, and more careful in what I said. I think I was in such an angry stage of grieving that I was unwilling to respect Mom's limits and unable to see that my actions would hurt her. I'm sure I also unconsciously wanted to rebel against feeling silenced all my life.

It has taken over five years to come back to a more comfortable relationship with Mom. For a long time I think she was afraid of what accusation would come out of my mouth next. She had good reason! Through therapy, I focused on accepting her and changing the way I behaved toward her. When I was able to let go of trying to force conversation about difficult issues, our whole rapport relaxed. I relied on my grief group to listen to the things she couldn't hear. At first I was angry about having to interact with Mom in a way that felt superficial to me, but I now understand her need to feel comfortable around me. By stepping back, I made room for both of us to reveal our feelings as we wish. When deeper conversations do come up now, unpredictably, I welcome them. They have brought us closer.

I'm glad that I could reach an adult understanding with Mom while she is still alive. You and I will never have that chance, Dad. It is only through your death that I can learn more about you. Some things I may never understand, and I must accept these contradictions. I always felt closest to the naturalist part of you that led us on long walks and spoke of "communing with nature" in the garden. I saw you deeply engaged with earth's cycles of abundant life and quiet decay, lovingly "putting the garden to bed" each fall by sowing cover crop, stacking corn stalks, and burying celery in straw. Yet how could you disrespect life so completely that you destroyed your own? How could you ignore your place in the delicate net of life that holds us all? Is suicide part of the natural cycle? I imagine you would say yes. To me it will always feel like a violent injury to all of life, a hole torn in the net.

The last entry in your garden journal, November 30, 1986, reads, "First killing frost, killing dahlias." Did you write that on the morning of the 30th, the day before you died, or did you walk out in the garden late that night and see the frost? Was this the sign you were waiting for? There is a strange symmetry, as well as vengefulness, about the time of year, and the date you chose to die: the end of the garden season, the beginning of the month, right between the two major winter holidays. Were you unable to face another Christmas season and the long gray months afterward?

You know it's not in the repertoire of our family to ask for help. Perhaps you didn't even realize you needed (or could find) help for your depression that winter. After your death, I didn't know I needed help either until I met with a grief counselor for the first time, thanks to a very persistent friend. I had no idea that a whole body of knowledge about suicide and grieving existed and that I could learn to heal from the loss of you.

Finding my footing as an artist and learning to live and create are now the greatest gifts of your death. In the last four years I have reached a point where I want to share with others what I've learned. This feeling has found its right form in ROOTS AND BRANCHES, an expressive arts program I created for the organization where I receive grief counseling. In the safe community of these classes, clients explore feelings and memories from new angles through writing, movement, and theater. They find that creativity reconnects them deeply to life. We received a grant to start the program in 1996 and are now moving strongly into the second year. I can truly say that designing and teaching in this program feels like what I am meant to do. One of my eighty-year-old students says, "This is the high point of my week. I wouldn't miss it. It is the only thing that lifts me up." I wish that you too had been able to let your creativity lift you out of despair. Making art embodies hope.

I want to offer my life as an example, an emblem of hope. If this story inspires others to reach for life, then I know I have done justice to the lessons of your death. I doubt you had any thought of what your death might mean, from the tar pit where you saw no options. But if you look now, you will see that I have taken your despair, narrowed to the pinpoint of a shotgun sight, callused with fear like a grenade, and made it into something beautiful.

We buried your ashes in the garden. It was after midnight, following the memorial service and the reception. I wore your garden boots and overcoat and still I was shivering. We brought flashlights, and I put some candles on the ground in paper bags so they wouldn't blow out. They made steady lamplike markers in the windy darkness of the garden that seemed as big as a field that night. Mom picked a spot where the corn, your most prized crop, had grown. She asked each of us to dig part of a short furrow with a spade. The soil, not yet frozen, was wet and heavy to my arms, like your body that I hadn't seen in death. The withered cornstalks were piled in neat rows like bolster pillows, and the winter rye had grown up, nearly covering the stalks. It felt strange to think that you had probably inspected all of these details on the day before you killed yourself, just a week ago.

We took turns spreading your ashes in the furrow, spilling them from the neatly wrapped cardboard box. I was startled to see so many fragments of bone. My eyes strained to recognize something, a piece of femur, a knuckle. I was still thinking like the archaeologist you had trained me to be. We each shoveled soil back into the trench. When we were done, the earth was mounded up slightly, like a planted row. This garden was so familiar to each of us, yet all of us together was not familiar any more, and what we were doing here not familiar at all. We stood still, staring down, not wanting to be finished. I knew what was missing. I walked slowly over the loose soil in your boots, pressing it toward the center, leaving slanted footprints down the row just as you would have done next spring.

Greacian Goeke

Greacian Goeke was thirty-three in 1986 when her father, aged sixty-nine, completed suicide.

ROOT AND BRANCHES is an extension of the Center for Elderly Suicide Prevention and Grief-Related Services, 3626 Geary Blvd., San Francisco, CA 94118, 415/750–5355. Patrick Arbore, executive director. The program received first-year funding from the California Arts Council. I am deeply grateful to Patrick Arbore and my fellow grief group members for seeing me through the past ten years.—G.G.

Of Fathers and Sons

Eventually, we have to leave the dead behind. There is nothing else we can do. Because the living need us more.

Facts first, then feelings. I am a thirty-three-year-old oldest son. In December 1994, my wife and I introduced my fifty-two-year-old father to his first grandchild, our son, then a month old. Seven weeks later, my father killed himself. He had no history of depression, and it appears that he developed an unexplained suicidal psychosis with no external psychological or physiological cause. I know that he must have been deluded when he did it, that the world he saw was not the real world. But two years later, the facts are still the facts.

Almost from the moment Dad died, I knew where I would have to get to. I would have to accept his death; accept it as suicide, learn to live with it, and finally move beyond it. I even found a book that listed seven stages of grief, neatly subdivided. I resented being that predictable. We like to think our experience is unique. But I knew that I wasn't unique, and I understood where I would have to go, although understanding isn't quite the same as doing. In the two years since he died I've traveled a long way. I know I have further still to go, and I don't know whether I've done the easy bit or the hard bit. But these days I spend most of my time in the place called "acceptance," which is at the end of all the lists I've read.

Some things are easier to accept than others. I accept that my father killed himself and that when he did it, he thought he was being rational and doing the best for his family. I expected that last idea would be really hard to accept, but it isn't. Not surprisingly, the hardest ideas to accept are the ones closest to me. For example, it is hard to accept that my father chose to kill himself seven weeks after first meeting his grandson.

This hurts my pride. I am proud of my son and of the way I am trying to raise him. I expected my father to be proud too, of him and of me. I wanted to show my dad something I could do really well, something he would appreciate and respect. And now I can't. I can't help feeling that his grandson should have mattered more to him, been enough to live for, even more than the rest of us should.

Equally hard to accept is that I still don't know if my son can trust me. I don't know that I can trust myself, or let anyone really trust me. My father was the most solid, reliable person in my life, reliable to the point of dullness, just as dads are meant to be — just as I want to be for my son. And then he killed himself. I tell my son as he sleeps that I will look after him, that I won't desert him. Or I try to tell him. Sometimes I can't even let myself say it.

On my good days (which are most days), I tell my son that I will do my best for him, and that's mostly good enough. On my good days, I agree with my wife, who says that I can only do my best, I am only human, and that all my son wants to know is whether I will be home at dinnertime. But on my bad days, I need to give him more certainty than that. When I'm alone with my son and I want him to feel safe, loved, and protected, what can I promise him? I'm sure when I was tiny, my dad made promises to me in the night. I expect he said more to me when I was two than when I was twenty. But he broke those promises, so what can I say to my son?

On my really good days, when I'm balanced and at peace with myself, I know that this bit of anxiety is really for my benefit, not my son's. That from my son's perspective, our relationship exists only on its own terms. I feel as if every time I describe or define that relationship in terms of a man he doesn't know, I waste emotional energy, energy that I should use to build a precious bond between us.

Sometime soon, I will start to explain his grandfather to him. I will tell him about his life and about his death. He'll be ready to hear that story soon, and I'll be ready to tell it. But before then, I have to leave the dead behind. There is nothing else I can do because the living need me more. This isn't to deny my father, only to acknowledge that he has no further need of me, unlike my son and the other people I love. When I describe my father to my son, I have to do it from the place where we who have chosen to live, live.

John F.

John F. was thirty in 1994 when his father, aged fifty-two, completed suicide.

The Process of Cultivating

For seventeen years, my father was a successful insurance salesman. He was often the top salesperson in a seventeen-state re-
gion. He was always a respected businessperson. But external
marks of success were not enough to quiet his anxious insecurities.
In 1972, Dad bought a dairy farm in Wisconsin and moved my
mother, me (then four years old), and my younger sister to a new
place and a new life. My father was as successful a dairy farmer as
he was an insurance salesman. Our farm consistently produced as
much milk as nearby farms with twice as many cows. Yet despite
his continued success and high standing in a new community, my
father began feeling alone and friendless. He continued to worry
excessively over normal debts and responsibilities.

I do not remember my father as depressed—although I know
now that he was the fourth generation of his family to suffer from
this. I do recall the stress created by the unrelenting demands of
his perfectionism and the simmering anger that possessed him
when life fell short of his expectations. I went to boarding school
in 1984, at the age of fourteen, to escape the uneasy atmosphere of
home. Looking back, I recognize signs of depression in him—especially after his mother died in 1986. At the time, such symptoms
were not clear to me.

After my grandmother died, Dad became more emotional. My
mother tried to talk with him, but limitations in her own experiences and abilities left her at her wit's end. At this time, she would
turn to me for assistance because "he does better after he talks with
you." During my years at boarding school, we established a comfortable relationship over the phone. So I became the phone therapist responsible for pulling my father out of his blackest depression.
I do not resent my mother for putting me in this position. I see it as

a way of keeping Dad's problems a matter of concern for the whole family, not just my mother. In retrospect, this was a reversal of the ordinary parent-child relationship, but at the time it was simply a continuation of a pattern of "looking after" my father.

If his mother's death drove my father deeper into depression, it was the revelation that I had been sexually abused by my mother's brother during my childhood that seemed to sink him. He was flooded with a sense of failure from which he never recovered. Although my father did not kill himself until six years after this news, I shoulder the burden of wondering whether my disclosure contributed to his death. Especially painful is the memory of having told him this terrible news in a time of anger. His reaction is a treasured memory. Instead of greeting this disclosure with the accusations that I feared, my father clutched me to him in sorrow.

In August 1991, I joined a Catholic religious order. My relationship with my father continued to grow. In December 1991, I shared with my family that I was gay. Once again, my father embraced me, but ultimately he had a hard time accepting such a countercultural lifestyle. I continued to talk with my father on the phone. He missed me terribly, which plunged him even further into his depression.

In November 1992, two days before Thanksgiving, my father did not show up for his daily farm chores. Considering his absolute fidelity to the farm, this was an unusual and worrisome event. The hired man and a neighbor searched for him. They discovered him in his bedroom—unconscious from an overdose of prescription medications. This was not an accidental overdose, but a deliberate attempt to end his life. My mother and sister were forced to admit him to the local hospital.

I was notified and rushed home from the novitiate ninety minutes away. After several discussions between the family and my father's doctor, we decided not to commit him to an institution for the mentally ill. Although this choice respected my father's wishes, in retrospect, I feel some anger toward the doctor for not providing greater guidance. This was also a time of crisis and anger with my father for his unwillingness to seek further help. Released from the hospital, my father returned home and tried, even in his weakened state, to resume his daily responsibilities. As much as I longed to stay at the farm and share my family's care for my father, my novitiate director insisted that I return. It was difficult to explain to the members of my community what had happened and to convince them of my need to stay home. My life was pulled in different directions by competing commitments.

During the week following my father's return home, I was in constant phone communication with him. These conversations gave me the opportunity to express the complex mix of emotions I was experiencing: anger, pain, love. When he persisted, "You will be better off without me," I protested all the louder, "I need you in my life."

This week of phone calls was in many ways an intensification of our usual relationship—me taking care of and stabilizing him. Through most of these conversations, I felt a vague sense of dread; a cold conviction that he would attempt suicide again. At the end of the week, I found myself feeling hopeful about the future. Indeed, I shared this optimism with my religious brethren during a weekend retreat I had to attend. (Again, a conflict in commitments. I would have preferred to be with my father, but my attendance was expected.)

On December 4, 1992, I learned of my father's death. His brother found him in the garaged truck, engine still running, with a gunshot wound in his chest. My uncle stopped the engine, and my father breathed his last breath—leaving this world in an act of love for his family. He left a letter addressed "To My Family" to assure us that he loved us and that we would be okay. Ever since then, time has been split into two eras: life before and life after December 1992.

When I arrived home, my tearful sister greeted me with the stark statement, "I have no one to walk me down the aisle." My mother declared, "I have no more husband." I was in a different place, beyond tears, expected to be the "strong one" who would take care of arrangements. It was a last gift to my father to plan his funeral service. It was rewarding to offer my family something during our time of greatest need. Although my responsibilities were gratifying, they prevented me from fully grieving. It was hard to grieve when it was so easy to take care of everyone. Since that time, I have learned that grief is neither short nor simple. Although my mother is not inclined to discuss Dad's death at length, I feel that she, my sister, and I have grieved our loss together. We have not indulged in distractions or finger pointing. The process of grief has changed us individually and as a family, but, thankfully, it did not rob us of the comfort of one another.

After the Monday burial, my religious order again pressured me to go against my own desires. Told to return to our novitiate on Friday instead of the Sunday I preferred, I seriously considered leaving the order then and there. My mother persuaded me not to make any drastic decisions during such an emotional time. I am glad that I took her advice. Making this decision later apart from the intense emotion of my father's death gave my choice an integrity that otherwise would have been lacking. With my mind only slightly at ease, I left the farm again. When I next returned, it was to oversee an auction of our farm, the cattle, and the machinery. Neighboring farmers came from far and near, on their own initiative after having worked in their own fields all day, to help prepare for the auction. They cleaned each piece of machinery with the same care that my father had shown for so many years. Working with their hands in this way was an expression of their love and respect for my father—and of their loss.

The auctioneer told us that he had never seen prices go so high—a testament to the years of hard work my father had invested. As I watched the cattle and machinery leave the farm, I experienced yet another loss and was forced to accept another transition.

I bear this in mind when I consider my father's last act. He could not envision the long-term consequences of his suicide for our family. Most likely, he was convinced that what he was doing would liberate us in some way. I am not burdened with the common survivor obsession, "Could I have prevented his suicide?" The thought that I could have stopped my father makes me into a hero and deprives him of choice. The challenge, as I see it, is to give my father permission to take his life, even if this action is one I protest. Sometimes I have imagined sitting with him during those final moments in the truck. I force myself to accept what he was about to do—for his sake.

Although I am no longer a child, I continue to need and invite my father's wisdom and guidance. Many times since his death, I have found myself thinking wistfully, "If only Dad were here, he would know what to do." During the months after my decision to leave the religious order, I was faced with a multitude of financial and practical matters that were foreign and often overwhelming to me. At such times, I was sharply aware of my father's absence. The combination of his loving heart and his business acumen would have served me well. Most likely my father would not have dealt well with my current relationship. Yet in some fashion, it was he who freed me to integrate my life more fully. Like those who take their lives, we all wake up one day and realize our own inner authority. On that day, we no longer care what other people think. What is important is what seems right to us.

After leaving the religious order while pursuing my master's degree in clinical social work, I gained yet another insight. In many ways a lifetime of being different (sexually abused, gay, raised on a farm, a member of a religious order) has served me well in dealing with my father's suicide. I have developed an acceptance of being different, which has formed my identity. Feeling marginalized enabled me to develop coping skills and a willingness to seek out professional counseling when needed. My identity of being different empowered me to accept my father's different kind of death.

As a mental health professional, I am aware of the genetic predisposition to depression to which I am heir; I am equally conscious of the crucial differences that set my father and me apart. In many ways I resemble my father—in physical appearance, habits, worries, loves. I understand that to identify with his destructive patterns would be to invite disaster. In light of this, I have made changes that will enable me to survive. For example, unlike my Dad, I see the world in shades of gray, rather than in black and white.

I consider my father's suicide symbolic of his life. The hands with which he cultivated the fields to provide for his family were the very hands by which he took his life. As a son who enjoyed a special relationship with this remarkable man, I can appreciate the fitness of his final act. When I ponder how I have survived the traumas of childhood sexual abuse and my dad's suicide, I know that it is because of the virtues Dad instilled in me: honesty, responsibility, perseverance. I have been asked whether it ever gnaws at me that the one who helped give me life took his own. It does not. My father planted many seeds, cultivated many fields, and reaped many fruits. The ripened fruit of one harvest to which he will never be witness lies in me. My father gave me life. I still have it—I have a life that is what it is because of who he was.

Paul J.

Paul J. was twenty-four in 1992 when his father, aged
fifty-one, completed suicide.

Flying Lessons

My father was an airline pilot and I was proud of him for doing what he loved. His parents had not wanted him to pursue aviation, but he persevered. His lesson taught me a lot about life: Do what you love. I remember my father having lots of energy and really enjoying himself when I was young. He sang and whistled. He had a happy marriage and two loving children. But my father drank too much even then.

He wasn't abusive when he drank. Somehow, this made it easier to ignore. My mom was concerned, but not overly so. At some point in his life his problems began to overcome him. He began to drink more. In time, his stress levels became so high that he had to stop flying. In 1974 he took a disability retirement from his airline. He was told to seek psychiatric help, but he refused. Several years later he said that the prospect of dying was less frightening to him than feeling the emotions he was numbing. He became suicidal. Once he said, "If it wasn't for my wife and children I would kill myself." The statement indicates his love for us, but it also pisses me off. It places a huge burden on the family—be there or Dad will shoot himself. One time when I was arguing with Dad he blurted out, "What do you want me to do . . . kill myself?" Then he walked outside, got in his car, and drove away. He came back that time. But there is still a part of my brain that believes that my strong emotions will cause someone to die. I struggle not to pass this distorted thinking on to my children.

During my teenage years, Dad seldom sang or whistled. He spent a great deal of time sitting in the kitchen and staring out the back window. He drank tea during the day. At night he drank beer or wine and watched TV until very late. I felt neglected and lonely. Since nobody told me what was going on, I thought I was the problem, and I became depressed. Each of us began to exist in our own little worlds. I alternated between denial and contemplating my own suicide. I lived with the fear that Dad would kill himself. Intuitively I knew I had to get out of there.

I first learned about the disease of alcoholism when I was at college. One day a pilot for a major airline came to our school (it was an aviation school) and spoke about his battle with alcoholism and his road to sobriety. Somehow his story penetrated my denial. I didn't seek help for myself right away, but I couldn't shake what that man told me. I finally began my own road to healing at the age of twenty-one . . . twelve years before Dad killed himself.

I often wonder why some people get help and begin living more vibrant lives while others just fade away. Over the last ten years, I was able to talk openly about the pain that I felt with my father and mother. It wasn't easy—skydiving for the first time was less intense. I told my father how hurt I would feel if he killed himself. For the first time in my life, I told him that I loved him. I tried many times to convince him to get help, but he never did.

I found out about my dad's death after I stepped off a plane I had copiloted from Detroit to St. Louis. The woman at the crew desk already knew and had set up my trip home. She looked at me with compassion and said, "I'm so sorry." She invited me behind the counter to avail myself of what little privacy there was. A fellow pilot responded with similar sensitivity. These people helped me because they had the strength to face death and were not put off by my intense feelings. They provided compassion, not problem solving; I needed to feel my feelings first and analyze them later. Many people were and are afraid to say anything about my father to me. Saddest of all, my father's family rarely mentions him. I try to speak about my dad first to let them know I am comfortable talking about him, but it doesn't advance the conversation.

One forum in which I can speak openly about my father and

my feelings about his death are Survivors of Suicide groups. Hearing the stories of others diminishes my sense of loneliness. I have found that if I miss a meeting or I haven't been able to talk about the suicide for a while I become irritable and tense. It would have been too burdensome to make my wife my entire support system. It was very hard for her to go through this loss with me. Some days, especially when she was sad about her own father who suffers from Alzheimer's disease, she just wasn't able to listen to my pain and sadness. In fairness to her and to us, I have made sure I ask others to listen to me too.

Part of what I've had to work out during the time since my dad's retirement and eventual suicide is what it means to be a man. In particular, I've needed to learn how to accept my feelings and to allow myself to cry. I feared that if I began to cry I wouldn't be able to stop. To my surprise, my tears have been the pathway to my healing. It has become very important to share my emotions with those who can handle them. When I am able, I let my wife hold me when I cry. Although I first had to overcome anxiety about the response of other men to my tears (I thought I would be perceived as a weak man), I have found letting them see my emotions to be very healing. I've realized that it takes strong men to buck societal norms and do whatever it takes to heal. Part of my motivation to develop healthier coping skills than my father had is my desire not to pass on destructive patterns to a new generation. But, despite all my growth, I am scared that when I become my father's age I will see and feel the type of pain that incapacitated him.

For some time, the most vivid image I had of my father was his exit from this world—an exit terrible in its specifics and its outcome. The pain this image evokes is beyond my capacity to describe. The pain of him dying alone. The pain of him not wanting to be a bother to anyone and his refusal to let people help him.

The pain of him not realizing how important his life was. I weep for his inability to know his connection to all people and all things. To help counter this traumatic image, I've concentrated on a memory I have of him from childhood. I was sitting next to him while he was working on a crossword puzzle. He had on a blue corduroy shirt. He smelled of pipe tobacco. Most clearly I remember his breathing. When I remember his breathing a sort of peace comes over me like it did when I was a child. I felt cared for, I felt safe. It is important for me to remember my father by how he lived his life, not by how he left it.

I often wonder what I can teach my children about the lessons of my childhood and the kind of man my father was. The most important thing I want my new daughter to know is that I love her and care about her. I also want her to know that when parents are sick, it is not her fault. I want to make it clear that she is free to share her feelings with me, even if that feeling is anger with me. As for how and when I will tell her about my father's death, I plan on telling her as soon as she asks or is curious about why she can't see him. We will tell her my dad had a disease that affected how he thought. His disease prevented him from realizing how important he really was to himself, to God, and to us. I will also tell her that he killed himself. Children are more capable of handling the truth than many people give them credit for. (It's the adults I worry about.) I will also share with her the wonderful things my father taught me and how much he loved little children.

I miss my father. Of all my current feelings, missing my father is the strongest. My father will never see any of his grandchildren. I will never be able to see him hold our newborn daughter. I can't hug him. I can't tell him I love him. I miss his laughter. I miss his flying stories. I often wonder why I chose to fly airplanes for a living. I didn't want to follow in my father's footsteps. At least not the depressed father I knew from my teenage years. But, I wonder if I did subconsciously choose it to find out why it once gave my father such joy. When I look with a sense of awe at a beautiful sunset from an airplane, I wonder if my dad can see it with me.

James A. Gessner

James A. Gessner was thirty-three in 1995 when his father, aged sixty-five, completed suicide.

Professional Life

While still reeling from the shock of all that had changed in my life, I returned to school a few days later. I had trouble concentrating on schoolwork and did not know how to deal with my grief away from my family. I experienced anxiety attacks whenever the subject concerned fathers, guns, or suicide. One attack was so bad that I left a child psychology lecture on fathers. One psychology professor did ask if he could help, but he didn't address my need to grieve. The end result was that I flunked out of college and lost any ambition I had for the future.

Susan Ford

With the help of a support group and therapy, the
author has since completed college.

I am a geriatric nurse. After my father's suicide, I found only pain in dealing with the elderly men I had once cherished. I had always laughed and joked with them and loved talking about their lives. Now I found that I kept a distance from them and avoided giving the hugs and special words that I had once given so freely—it was too distressing a contrast with the lack of a lovely old man in my life.

Mary Ann Schmidt

Life without a Parent

A year after my mother took her life I was on my way to work. It was raining, and I was at the bus stop. In its wetness, the rain got the best of me. I began crying. I wasn't thinking of anything in particular at the time, but my body felt "loss." There was another woman at the bus stop. She had gray hair. At first I tried hiding my grief, then I couldn't contain it. Finally we made eye contact. In that moment, I don't know how it happened, I fell into her open arms. She held me for a few minutes and patted my back. She said, "You're going to be okay." She didn't ask me what was wrong. That event helped heal me. There are many others, and they continue to come along when I'm receptive to them.

JoDe Rimar

Sometimes I am lonesome for the only person with a mother knowledge of me. Just because I'm thirty-five doesn't mean I don't miss my "mommy."

Margo McDaniel

My father's suicide made me feel abandoned for two reasons. First, I had struggled with my relationship with my father for most of my life. Only three years prior to his death we had begun a friendship between father and daughter. I had just learned that he was a compassionate, sensitive man. He had become an important male figure in my life. His final act robbed me of continuing a beautiful and meaningful relationship, of the possibility of knowing my father. Second, he left me eleven weeks before he was to walk me down the aisle at my wedding—a special moment and transition in my life. Since we had finally developed a friendship, it would have been a meaningful honor for him to participate in my wedding. Even though my brothers escorted me down the aisle, I felt a deep sense of loss and emptiness when I remembered my father's elected absence.

Carrie P. Riley

III

*Perspectives on a
Common Loss*

Uncommon Grace

My mother carried herself with an elegance and refinement that was at once compelling and elusive. Even among intimates, she maintained a reserved manner. Hence, when depression ravaged her mind and her spirit, a certain Blanche DuBois air of tragedy hung over her ordeal. Foreshadows of my mother's depression appeared during the summer of 1986. But when the full-fledged illness descended, it came on suddenly and immediately reduced her to a childlike state. Within a short time we realized that she required more care than we could provide, and we admitted her to the psychiatric ward of a local hospital. I will never forget how she gripped my hand as we sat through the nurse's intake, how frightened she looked, how hard I cried. Thus began our four-year cycle of hospitalizations and releases, psychiatrists and psychologists, drugs and therapies, a cycle that alternated between Indianapolis (my hometown) and Philadelphia (my mother's hometown).

This repeated moving between two "homes," between two families (her spouse and children in one place, her five siblings in the other), took its toll—on her in the form of interrupted treatments and the impossibility of extended family counseling; on us as we disagreed about the best course of care for her. The family, nuclear and extended, became torn over the form and location of her therapy. I became the loudest agitator for her to stay in Indiana and receive a combination of drug and counseling therapy there. In the spring of 1990, she did so and initially she did very well; she was the best she had been in years. But in September, she began sliding into the abyss again. On Sunday, November 11, 1990, while my father was at church and my youngest brother overnight at a friend's, she went down into the cold garage and ended the pain that had become her life.

That morning, Louis, my husband of a little more than a year, and I were preparing to walk to our church when the phone rang. I answered the phone and could tell by my father's tone that something awful had happened. After literally reeling from the terrible news, I entered into a strange calm; I packed our bags and Louis arranged for friends to look after our place. During the drive to Indianapolis, I alternated between hope that she would make it, fear that she would not, and panic at the possibility that she was already dead. We were silent the entire distance. When we turned onto our street, our driveway was full of cars. But it was not until I walked in the side door and saw my then twenty-year-old brother Chris turn to me with swollen eyes that I knew the worst had happened. We clung to each other and sobbed. I could not sleep that night; worn out from crying all afternoon and evening, I cried no more, but I imagined that if I could keep vigil through the night somehow she would come back to us.

Many survivors of suicide report that they remember little of the week of the funeral and burial of their loved one. For me, the opposite is the case. I remember those events in excruciating detail. I recall performing all the attendant duties of death and the unbearable pain each one brought with it; choosing her coffin (blue because it was her favorite color), her burial plot (near a pond because she loved the ocean), the clothes she would wear, the readings and songs for her funeral Mass. Around the kitchen table, where my family had shared so many laughter-filled meals, were now my grief-bowed siblings and myself discussing which flowers we wanted for her casket. The decisions that had to be made gave us something to focus on, something to do for our mom and yet it was an unreal, surreal time.

But I also recall the luminous moments of that week when I was awed by the outpouring of love and support we received. Our phone rang constantly. The mail carried messages of warmth and support across the miles. Friends and neighbors poured in with sympathy and meals. We began a running joke about the "Ham-o-Meter," which recorded how many ham dinners we were given. I remember my then seventeen-year-old brother Joe surrounded by twenty or more high school friends in our basement. They came and went throughout the week, skipping class to be with him. Their presence, their youth, and obvious yet awkward concern, was somehow comforting to everyone. Each of us had friends come from long distances—one of mine traveled eighteen hours on a train, some of my parents' friends traveled all night—to be with us. My friends were an endless source of strength throughout Mom's long illness (an illness few of them understood) and have continued to be so. I would not have survived without them.

My husband has enabled me not only to survive but to reconnect with the joys of life. My mother's death was the first death that Louis had experienced; it is not the introduction to death that I would have wished for him. Caught unaware and unprepared to respond to the raw intensity of my grief, Louis rose magnificently to the occasion. When I registered to participate in an eight-week survivors of suicide group, he volunteered to join me. It would, he explained, give him a greater understanding of my loss and my sorrow. To my knowledge, he is the only spouse of a survivor to attend such sessions. Sharing these meetings gave us a common context for my loss, for our loss. Without the support group, I fear that our differing responses would have alienated us. In the immediate months and even years after Mom's death, my overriding emotion was sadness, for Louis it was anger. He was angry at Mom "for doing this" to his wife, he was angry with Mom for denying him the opportunity to come to know her. With the wisdom of the support group, we accepted our reactions as equally legitimate expressions of grief.

Most distressing during these early months were occasional thoughts of committing suicide myself. I suspect that some of my suicidal thoughts came not so much from the unbearableness of my sorrow as from an attempt to identify more closely with my mother, to try to understand what she felt and thought as she descended the stairs to the garage. Efforts to reconstruct imaginatively the circumstances of her death coupled with the desire to be with her drew me into a sympathetic suicidal mentality.

Consciously, I stopped myself because I did not want to subject my husband to the ordeal of discovering my body. Subconsciously, I think I hesitated because I was aware, however inchoately, that my siblings needed me to help them come to terms with their grief; that they, my husband, father, and friends should be spared any more unnecessary pain; and that life might somehow still hold meaning and joy for me and my family again. I did not directly tell anyone about these suicidal thoughts, although I hinted at them to my husband and a few close friends. I felt everyone had enough to worry about. In retrospect, it would have been wise to share these frightening thoughts with someone. Best if it had been a counselor, someone removed from my personal situation and trained to assess real risk. As it was, once I learned from reading that such thoughts were not uncommon among survivors, I was less fearful that I would actually act on an impulse.

One area of concern to me that I did not find addressed in anything I read was that of sexuality. Certainly some accounts mentioned "decreased interest in sex" as one of the hallmarks of depression but nothing beyond that. For me, the first few months after Mom's death were marked not just by decreased interest in sex but by tremendous emotional upheaval respecting it. Sex is a profound symbolic affirmation of life, and it is difficult to affirm life when someone you love has recently negated it. Moreover, for me, it triggered specific associations with my loss. Its intimacy reminded me that I would never again share moments of closeness with my mother; its physicality highlighted the loss of her touch, her voice. Confident that as the intensity of my grief subsided, this aspect of our relationship would normalize, we weathered this unexpected stress on our young marriage.

A related strain was caused by our suddenly divergent opinions regarding having children. The possibility of having children raised a number of issues for me. I wondered, if we have children, "How will I cope with the fact that they will never know their grandmother? How will we tell them about what happened? When do we tell them about what happened? How much do we tell? Will they be born with a predisposition to depression and suicide?" This last question haunted me the most because, in addition to my mother's illness, we had other family members with a history of depression. A friend who was studying psychology at the time helped me learn more about the possibility of a genetic predisposition to depression. After hearing the evidence, I felt reassured that although there is a possible link, it is not inevitable. Moreover, as my husband noted, if you know your family history disposes you to a condition, be it physical or mental, you educate yourself. If you suspect that the condition is manifesting itself, seek immediate professional help.

For nearly a year after Mom died, however, I was convinced that I no longer wanted children. When I voiced my decision not to have children to my friends, they were stunned. For as long as they had known me, indeed for as long as I could remember, I had happily anticipated becoming a mother. How could such an enduring desire be extinguished? Simple—motherhood held appeal to me because my own mother was so wonderful at it, but when she died all the joy I associated with the concept of "mother" died too. As I grew up, I experienced and became increasingly conscious of how much she enjoyed her role as mother, and I looked forward to sharing with my own children the love she lavished on her four children. I kept locked in my memory the little things she did that held special meaning to me—surprising us with theme cookies on every holiday (major and minor), collecting five new Christmas tree ornaments each year (one for each child and one for the family). I waited eagerly for the day when I would pass these traditions on within my own family. But it was more than these rituals I wanted to hand on. I wanted to re-create the tender, laughter-filled atmosphere that she brought to our home. But when she took her life, the depth of positive feeling I associated with being a mother transformed, literally overnight, into an aversion to all things related to motherhood. It was just too painful to contemplate anything connected with mothers, especially being one myself. Part of what effected this transformation was, I believe, my sense that by committing suicide Mom repudiated all the values she embodied: hopefulness, patience, perseverance, serenity. This one act destroyed my confidence in these values and all my dreams of being a mother, like my mother, who conveyed these to her children.

Although I did not vocalize this change in my feelings often, Louis was well aware that it lurked beneath the surface. He saw my tears when expectant friends told of shopping for baby clothes with their mothers, when grandmothers chatted with their daughters while the grandchildren climbed contentedly into their laps. And while he always let me know I could discuss this issue with him whenever I wanted or needed to, he never, bless him, forced a confrontation over it. I think he knew that in time this particular wound would heal and my desire to have a family would reemerge. For eight months after Mom's death, I consciously avoided situations in which I would need to interact with children or proud mothers who wanted to share their child's latest accomplishment with me. This was a way to protect myself from the maelstrom of emotion that such encounters inevitably produced. But soon after, during a visit with my sister, I met a little boy who captured my heart and revived my dreams of motherhood.

In light of my agony about whether or not to have children after my mother's suicide, it is bitterly ironic that two years after my mother's death my husband and I found ourselves struggling with infertility. Our experience resurrected intense emotions about my mother's death. It has caused me, once again, to reintegrate this loss into the changing features of my life. As we have grieved the multiple losses of infertility, I became angry with my mother for the first time. I was mad that she, of her own volition, was not here when I desperately needed her. For the first time, I perceived myself as abandoned by her, and I responded with rage.

But more than anger, the overriding emotion in relation to my mother's suicide that infertility stirred was guilt. The day after we buried my mother, a relative told me that had I not insisted on her coming back to Indiana she would be alive today. Hearing these words shook me to my core. They reverberated with my own unspoken sense of guilt and responsibility. For months, I struggled with my relative's words of blame and my own self-accusation, but by the time I was dealing with infertility two years later, they were, for the most part, a faint echo. But with this second crisis upon me, their volume rose to a deafening din. I interpreted my inability to bear children as proof of my guilt, as the punishment for "causing" my mother's death. Who was meting out this punishment? Not God—but nature perhaps, or, in dreams, even my mother. It was as though the cosmos was exacting from me the capacity to give life in exchange for my part in taking my mother's. This destructive line of thinking was so powerful because it was largely unconscious. Only with the gentle prodding of a wise counselor was I able to unravel this twisted tale, bring it to light, and attempt to resolve it. Without doubt, my mother's suicide is a, if not the, major touchstone in my life, and subsequent events tend to be understood in terms of it. In this case, I sought desperately for some meaning of one traumatic experience in terms of an earlier one. Understandable, but unhelpful and misguided.

Now, as we eagerly await the adoption of our first child, the intense anger toward Mom has faded, but I remain convinced that whatever the circumstances, things would be all right if only she were here. It is a comfort to me that my own experience will enable me to empathize better with our child. Losing my mother through suicide has pressed me to engage issues similar to those with which adopted children grapple: the absence of the biological mother, a sense of rejection and abandonment by her. I hope that my sensitivity to these painful aspects of life will serve my child well.

As happy as my anticipation of our adoption is, it not surprisingly accentuates losses occasioned by Mom's death. Conscious that children often interpret their names as symbols of parental expectations, we have chosen not to name a daughter after my mother. This is a wrenching sacrifice for me. I would love to honor my mother and to connect her in this special way to the grandchild she will never know. But I knew my mother beyond her illness and death. I fear that a child who only perceives her grandmother through family reminiscences will be unable to situate the dramatic means of her death within a larger context of her life. I fear that my mother's name could be a source of destructive emulation.

The adoption also reminds me anew that after her death I have, in many ways, lost her entire side of the family. There is only occasional and strained contact with my mother's siblings. My child will not enjoy the large extended family I did. I try to remain close to those relatives who have reached out, and I learn to live with the absence of those who cannot come to terms with Mom's death as ultimately her act. I keep in contact (Christmas cards, an occasional note or call) in order to keep the door open to new possibilities, but in general I live my life without expecting them ever to be a full part of it again.

Compensating, albeit incompletely, for this loss is the enriched relationships I enjoy with my siblings. Mom's death has effected an intimacy among us that surpasses the ordinary. This is not to say that we have experienced her death uniformly. The brothers have suggested that we sisters have fixated on Mom's death; the sisters have suggested that the brothers have given it insufficient reflection. There's probably an element of truth in each observation. More complicated is the realization of how great were the differences in our relationships with Mom given our relative ages. I am conscious of the advantages of being firstborn: She was healthy throughout my childhood and adolescence; she attended all but one of my academic graduations; she was present at my wedding; we had the time to develop a more mature relationship. Sometimes the benefits of being eldest—of having what my siblings, especially my brothers, were denied—generates significant discomfort, even embarrassment, for me. At other times, I am angry with Mom for the legacy of absence she bequeathed to the others. It was crushing to learn that my youngest brother sometimes listens to a tape made in 1977 to hear how Mom sounded when she was well—he has no memories of those days.

Being the oldest child and a female, I wrestle with an impulse to provide mothering to my siblings. During times of difficulty for them and at the holidays, I must check my inclination to act the mother. Ultimately, this desire is frustrated by the reality that in the end I am their sister and nothing more. Their loss is as final as mine. Only recently did my sister suggest that we were each seeking from the other the best parts of our relationships with Mom— and repeatedly coming up short. Although this insight provides a sounder basis for our relationship, it required another mournful leave-taking of our mother. Perhaps it was this additional goodbye that prompted us finally to resize Mom's engagement and wedding rings for us to wear. It is a comfort to know Mom is tangibly with each of us every day.

Despite the differences and missteps in our sibling relationships, our common loss has become our greatest bond. Only we four know what it is to lose our mother. When everyone else has lost interest, we four are there to listen, day or night, to cry or to laugh. Our shared dark senses of humor have buoyed us on even the bleakest of days. For example, during my mother's wake, we were confronted with the harsh reality that people will make insensitive comments after someone has died, even more insensitive remarks after that person has died unexpectedly, and the most insensitive responses if that person committed suicide. To cope with the barrage of inane comments we ran an imaginary raffle for "Least Sensitive Comment." The winner was to receive one of our many hams. We would find each other during the wake and whisper, "I've got a runner-up," or "New first place here."

Our relationships are not dominated by Mom's suicide, but they are shaped by it—in ways wonderful and worrisome. On the bright side of the ledger, I suspect that it is our experience with sudden and tragic loss that inclines us to be in greater contact with one another than most adult siblings I know. Those of us on e-mail converse daily, we all converse weekly by phone; regular in-person visits are carefully coordinated and arranged. The increased frequency and depth of interaction is a tribute to Mom's talents as a mother. The shadow side is the latent fear that one of us will succumb to Mom's fate. An extended blue mood is cause for concern; actual bouts of depression are cause for alarm. We no longer harbor the naive presumption that things work out for the best. The reality of our mother's illness and suicide haunts our relationships and heightens our sensitivity, perhaps overly so, to any hints of such despair in one another. We must remind ourselves that most stories of depression do not end as Mom's did.

It is only recently that our father has begun to speak openly with us about our mother, her illness, and death. In general, however, I feel more comfortable talking with my siblings about Mom. Sometimes I keep our conversations private because I need the comfort of a fellow child's perspective. Other times, it is out of concern that my father and his new wife not feel awkward. Still others, it is because the subject is so new between me and my father. For me, my father was most supportive immediately after Mom's death. When I numbly repeated to him the terrible blaming words of one relative, he asked, "Did you do everything you could for her? Was it in her best interest as you understood it? Was it out of love? Because if it was out of love then you could have done no more. We are called to act out of love, nothing more." This comforted me and has given me pause for reflection over the years. But as the months passed, our different perceptions of Mom's death — for him, it was a foreseen outcome of her past relentless depression; for me, an unanticipated blow to hopes of her future recovery — hindered attempts to share our experiences. For me, his remarriage has both eased and complicated this effort. His wife is comfortable acknowledging my mother and her role in our family. This openness invites me to remember her aloud. However, she and my father sometimes underestimate the pain inherent for me in their relationship — that they are together means my mother is no more, my family as I knew it is no more.

Without qualification, my mother's mental illness and death are the worst things that have happened to me. And I venture that they will always retain this dubious honor. The suffering that her death caused is a perverse measure of my love for her. Although I would gladly renounce the pain and any wisdom her death has engendered, I would not surrender it if it means also laying aside that love. I carry on, not because I must (surely suicide gives the lie to this sentiment), but because I choose to. My life is radically and permanently altered by my mother's suicide, but it remains a life of gratitude because my mother was a woman of uncommon grace, and such grace endures.

Mary Stimming

Mary Stimming was twenty-six in 1990 when her mother, aged fifty-seven, completed suicide.

Endings and Beginnings

When I feel the warmth of the sun, or take a hike and witness the breathtaking beauty of the world, I am awed by the power of life. And I miss my mother. When I have an awful day or feel discouraged, I search for inner strength to find hope. And I miss my mother. No longer a child, I still yearn for her comfort and support, her warm touch and caring smile. Not feeling quite "grown up," I wish I had her advice when I ponder future plans or want to lessen my anxieties. I am like a boat adrift—missing the land I have left behind and seeking a harbor to feel safe and anchored. I have passed through rough waters.

For nearly five years prior to her death, my mother suffered from clinical depression. Her mental illness came in frenzied cycles; it smothered the spirit of the person she was and extinguished her hopes for the future. Prior to the onset of her depression, my mother was a healthy and caring woman whose generosity knew no bounds. She became ill during my freshman year at college, and though there were glimpses of the woman I knew during my childhood and adolescence, I never regained my "mother" once she became depressed. The years of her mental illness haunt me and in many ways were more difficult than the years since her death. I rarely speak of the constant fear, frustration, and helplessness that I felt from taking care of my mother. In a strange way, her suicide created an emotional outlet through which I could grieve. Though many people empathized with my situation during college, it wasn't until her physical death that her loss became tangible. I was then able to relate to others the depths of my pain concerning her absence—when I had actually been missing her for years.

My mother killed herself while I was serving in a volunteer program in Seattle, WA. Initially, the belief that my mother finally was at peace made her suicide easier to accept. But time and the emptiness I have felt since her death have eroded those pacifying thoughts. There is a strange practicality to death. Here I was making plane reservations and rescheduling my work responsibilities when my world had just collapsed. I was struck both by how kind people are: the outpouring of support from friends, people who came to my house that night or called—some who never even knew my mother. In fact, I thought the airlines had a code for "bereaved" by my name on their computer because everyone was so helpful to me on my trip home for the funeral. But I was also amazed at the indifference of the world. The most influential person to me, the one who gave me life and in whom I found endless acceptance, ceased to exist. And yet the clocks kept running, people went to work, and for the vast majority of humanity November 11, 1990, was like any other day. But it was not, and will never be that way for me.

As the central figure in our family, my mother's depression and suicide obviously affected our family dynamics. My siblings and I were close growing up. I treasure the memories of the many trips we took to the Jersey shore to vacation with our cousins and our mother's family. The first year of my mother's depression tore apart our sense of normalcy and threatened to destroy our sense of connectedness. We each sought to find reasons for why she became ill, and unfortunate blaming ensued. The later years of her depression and her suicide cemented our bonds with one another. Friends will often comment on how we seem to have our own unique language or way to relate with one another when we are together. The most ironic aspect of our present closeness is that throughout her life my mother strove for such closeness among her children. In her death she achieved all that she had hoped for us during her life. Without a doubt, the love, understanding, and dark sense of humor my siblings and I share has enabled me to see the light at the end of the tunnel (and trust that it is not an oncoming train).

My sister is my closest friend and was my strongest ally during my mother's depression and my personal journey since her suicide. But the emotional toll of these events has also caused intense conflict between us. I struggle between wanting to relate to her as a sister and yet longing for the maternal guidance that is missing in my life. I know that my sister will, and has, taken on the traditional role of mother for me during significant events of my life. But as much as I want her involvement, it also points out to me what I am missing, whom I am missing. Though she can never fill that void, I am thankful for her presence and for her sensitivity to how our mother's death has forever altered our lives.

Growing up, my brothers and I shared similar interests and temperaments that enabled us to relate to one another as friends and not solely as siblings. But when our mother became depressed, I unfairly blamed them because I wanted to find a reason for why she became ill. They were both still at home, and I did not have the intimate knowledge that they did of how her mental state had begun to deteriorate. I fear that my brothers may harbor resentment toward me because I was away at college during most of my mother's depression, and I was away from home when she killed herself.

It hurts me greatly when I hear of their struggles coping with her loss. As an older sister, I want to shelter them from this pain. This tendency to assume a protective or parental role has caused difficulties in the past, as my brothers perceived me as treating them as subordinates and not peers. This was amplified when I took over household responsibilities while my mother received treatment at hospitals and even when she was at home but unable to care for herself. Currently, we have resumed our style of relating as friends and have become even closer in the process.

The predominant feeling that I associate with my mother's suicide is sadness. But when I fear for my siblings' safety because she made suicide an "option" for us, I feel angry. Before the wake, we made a decision to be honest with those who may not have been aware of our mother's depression and inform them, if inquired, of the manner of her death. We agreed that we wanted to have no family secrets and that we wanted to dispel the stigma surrounding mental illness and suicide. I am grateful for that decision. Our open communication has allowed us to share with one another when we need help and to point out how our mother's suicide affects our behavior when we may not be aware of it individually. We know that we are in a higher risk group for depression and suicide. But we feel that we lessen that risk by our decision to educate ourselves and be constantly aware of threats to our well-being.

My relationship with my dad was complicated prior to the onset of my mother's depression. He has been, and continues to be, endlessly supportive of me. However, my mother was my "translator," understanding my emotions and mood changes better than anyone else. When she became ill, I lost my voice, particularly in relating with my father.

Shortly after my mother's death, my dad began dating. My initial reaction was shock. I was taken aback because it came so quickly and because it served as a reality check—my mother was truly gone. I was angry at my father for many reasons: It seemed that he was able to replace my mother and move on but I could not; I felt pulled out of the intense grief over my mother's death too soon and was forced to focus on the sudden changes of the present. But the most difficult aspect of my father's dating was his inability to understand why I was upset. It was not with intent, but it seemed beyond his ability to grasp the symbolism of his dating. And worse, my mother, whom I felt would have understood the ramifications of his actions, was not there to comfort me.

My father remarried in the fall of 1994. His wife is in a no-win situation. Even if she was a living saint I would find fault with her for not meeting the standards set by my mom. In truth, she is a kind woman who in many ways is more compatible with my father than my mother was and who has shown marked sensitivity to the awkwardness of her role. It would be easier if she was an "evil step-mother" so that I would feel justified in my ambivalence toward her. I no longer need "a mother," but I still search for the maternal influence and comfort that role could provide.

This search for the maternal has prompted me to foster relationships with the mothers of several of my friends. There is, however, a catch to this situation. I am grateful to have been taken in by so many families and cared for by these wonderful women. Yet, I am sharply aware that my relationships with them pale next to the real thing when I witness their interactions with their true daughters.

It is this realization that makes thinking about potential events in my future more difficult. Regardless of how pleasurable an event in my life is, it will always be tinged with sadness by the absence of my mother. Every birthday, every accomplishment was recognized by my mother. Likewise, after every disappointment, I was given unconditional support and compassion. I hope to get married, have children, and work in a fulfilling career. Yet when I think of these possibilities, I think of not having a mother beside me to help with wedding plans, of my children never knowing their grandmother, of missing my mother's support and guidance throughout my work experience. I believe that I will find contentment in my life and that I have many positive experiences to anticipate. However, they will be bittersweet without my mother there to share them.

To this day I feel disbelief about all that has transpired since my mother's depression. There are times when the pain is so overwhelming that I feel like her suicide happened yesterday. Then there are days that my consciousness of her absence is less acute. But the effects of her loss always linger somewhere. The most obvious time that I must confront her absence is when I return home. My visits to Indianapolis have lessened as there are too many painful reminders of how that city's significance to me has changed. I try to visit her grave often, but it seems to remove me even further from the reality of her loss. I have never cried at her grave. That site is not representative to me of who my mother was, just as the last few years of my mother's life were not a true depiction of the person she was or the life that she led.

The cemetery is still significant to me, however, as it is her final place of respite. At the burial, my father choked on his words as he told why we chose that particular plot. It was close to a pond, and my mother loved the water. He then spoke of her love for her siblings and friends and of the fulfillment she felt from her life. But, he said, it was her love of her children that gave her the greatest pleasure. She cherished her role as mother. As I stood there beside her casket, knowing his words to be true, I felt the deepest sense of emptiness and pain. If my mother truly loved me, and I know she did, then how could she leave me?

This gnawing question surfaces most during my darkest moments. It underlies my disturbing dreams and makes me challenge all that I once held as basic truths. I do not know the answer. I believe that her suicide was to give her refuge from her pain and that true to her self-sacrificing nature, it was to spare her family the agony of witnessing her paralyzing depression. But my mother did not die after a long, courageous battle from cancer. She was not tragically taken before her time by accident or by another's hand. My mother chose to end her life. And though I do not believe that she was in a rational state of mind as she descended the stairs into our garage, at some level she knew. She knew that she would no longer watch her children grow up or be a part of our future. While I can empathize with why my mother took her life, when I think of my pain since her death my sadness turns to anger. I cannot believe that she gave up all that she loved. All whom she loved. I feel abandoned.

Complicating my situation is the overlap between my personal life and my professional career in the field of mental health. I was a psychology major in college (oh, the joys of going to abnormal psychology class when you can claim more experiential knowledge than your professor). The volunteer position that I held when my mother committed suicide was as a counselor in a residential program for mentally ill adults. I was hesitant to accept this position because of my mother's history, and I was even more apprehensive about returning to my job after her death. Several of the clients I worked with were depressed, and many were either actively suicidal or had been recently hospitalized for attempting suicide. I was concerned about being overloaded with suicide and not being able to help my clients effectively. Fortunately, returning to a staff that has been trained to be sensitive to mental illness and the effects of suicide made my return to work as smooth as possible. Nevertheless, the central issues that confronted me then continued to present themselves in my postgraduate studies and in future employment.

My decision to enter graduate school in a counseling psychology program was based on my motivation to help others and to continue the work I so enjoyed in Seattle. Looking back, I am certain that my career choice and subsequent employment positions were strongly influenced by my role during my mother's depression and by the effects of her suicide. During the first year of graduate school, I was flooded with intense memories and feelings associated with my mother's death. After strong encouragement from my supervisor, I entered therapy to help me cope with past events and to learn to separate my personal issues from those of my clients. This experience also helped me reconnect with the totality of my mother—the grace, warmth, and loving spirit that I knew as a child—while also accepting the pain of the changes within her during the later years of her life. Over time, I became more comfortable balancing the interplay between my personal experiences and professional path. I recognized that I could turn my pain into a strength and not a liability in my career.

My most recent position was rooted in my own loss. For several years I worked as a child and family therapist in an economically depressed area. I hoped that as I was helped by others during my worst hours, so too could I help these children. Many of the children I worked with had been exposed to violence both at home and in their neighborhoods. Though they exhibit an amazing resiliency, they are scarred by loss and the potential threat of loss. Their vulnerability forced me, once again, to confront my own issues concerning my mother's death. The last year of my job found me struggling to save or protect the kids with whom I worked. Though these may be typical feelings for anyone working with children, for myself, it revived guilt about not being able to save my own mother. Because my mother's illness did not end "successfully," I know that my efforts similarly may fail. I strive to do everything "right" so that I will never again have to live through something so terribly wrong.

Leaving this position allowed me an opportunity to experience loss and grief differently than I have previously. I emphasized to others that because of the students' past exposure to abandonment and loss it was important how I terminated therapy with my caseload. But I also needed to recognize that my own past experience demanded careful attention to this task as well. This transition enabled me to see that loss can be creative, not just destructive.

My future plans are to continue working in a people-oriented field and to use my therapeutic skills in a less direct-service position. I foolishly envision finding a job that prompts no reminders of my mother's illness or suicide. But it is impossible to separate who I am from what I do, and so I hope that my future career allows me to help others, but not at the cost of my own best interests.

This professional change is difficult. In fact, since my mother's illness and suicide, all transitions are particularly difficult. Prior to her depression, my mother provided the stability and support that made previous passages manageable. Without her, changes are now anxiety provoking. My anxiety exists not only because of her absence, but also because I have seen that changes don't always happen for a reason or work out as planned. Because my mother's depression and death were so unexpected, I feel that I must always be prepared (emotionally, financially, etc.) for any possibility—especially the worst ones. This feeling was amplified by the death of several close relatives within the year following my mother's suicide. I am working to find a more balanced perspective on change and to feel more comfortable with uncertain outcomes.

One set of changes I've embraced since my mother's death is how I relate to others. When I was younger, I was often compared to my mother because we both tended to keep our feelings to ourselves and be better listeners than talkers. But when my mother became depressed, I made a conscious effort to express myself more openly, hoping to avoid her fate. Fortunately, I have been blessed by an amazing support system of friends who are willing to listen to my repetitive story, and they give me strength and encouragement when I am in need.

Being vulnerable to others is an ongoing process. My heartrate quickens when I sense conversation heading toward my family. I often employ humor when I become uncomfortable discussing my mother's depression or suicide. An adaptive coping mechanism, my humor can also distance me from my true feelings or create the illusion that I am coping with my situation in a stronger manner than I feel internally.

Entering therapy, sharing more of my emotions, and writing this essay are tools that I have used to come to terms with my mother's suicide. Though therapeutic, this essay was difficult to compose because I do not believe that I can accurately catalogue all that her death means to me. And the frequent revisions I have made reflect my fear that by finishing this essay, I misleadingly imply that I am similarly resolved with my mother's death. I know that I am not finished coming to terms with her suicide. But to me, being a "survivor" does not mean that I have placed this event and its effects behind me. It means a willingness to continue to struggle with the past, to live in the present, and to be open to the future.

The change from summer to fall is a poignant time for me as preparations for the long, cold winter coincide with the anniversary of my mother's death. Despite this convergence, I love the fall. The trees shed their vibrant leaves, and nature retreats in the hopes of blooming again. I too hope for renewal as I venture forth into a new cycle of my life without the guiding hand that nurtured me and gave me roots.

Maureen Stimming

Maureen Stimming was twenty-two in 1990 when her mother, aged fifty-seven, completed suicide.

It's the Story of a Lovely Lady

The first sixteen years of my life were like an episode of *The Brady Bunch*, except I like to think we were slightly better dressers. My two older sisters, younger brother, and I grew up in a loving, supportive, religious family. We lived in one of the most prestigious neighborhoods in Indianapolis, attended the best schools in the city, and went to the local Catholic church every Sunday. Dad had an executive job at a Fortune 100 company, and Mom stayed home with the kids. The strangest part of my youth was that my family was so normal. None of us were ever molested, there were no alcoholic or abusive parents, no affairs, divorce, or any other typical dysfunction. Of course, we had our occasional feuds among siblings and maybe some innocent trouble at school, but I rarely remember my parents even fighting. I've always thought of myself as extremely fortunate to have grown up in such a "model" family. To this day, I find it difficult to fathom how lucky my first sixteen years were. Up until my sophomore year of high school, life was just like the Bradys'.

But sometime in 1986 our family changed forever. Our family began a long and painful battle with my mother's depression. I wasn't even aware of her initial decline until one summer day, as I walked out the door for tennis, I found my oldest sister and mother in our den. My mother's suitcase was packed, she looked pale and hollow, as though she had been robbed of inner spirit. My sister told me, "Mom hasn't been feeling very well lately, and we're going to check her into the stress center." I asked a few questions and left. I remember arriving at the tennis center, parking my car, and hesitating for a few minutes as the news began to hit me. The radio was on, but I heard nothing as I began to cry with an overwhelming feeling of anxiety. After another minute or two, I took a deep breath, put my sunglasses on, and went out to the courts to teach the afternoon session with the skill of only the greatest of actors. I look back now and find this episode the foreshadowing of how I would deal with my mother's depression and, eventually, her suicide.

For five years my mother battled with depression. Treatment started with admission to the local hospital, where she worked with various psychologists. Shortly after, she was prescribed various antidepressant drugs. Her situation was distinctive in that, after unsuccessful treatment in Indianapolis, she began treatment with a leading expert on depression in Philadelphia. She was from Philly, and her siblings still live there. Since the doctor in Philadelphia had a reputation as one of the world's foremost authorities on depression and had recently published a popular book on the subject, we knew she was getting the best care possible. But we began a cycle of "Mom's depressed, send her to Philly, Mom's doing better, let's try things at home in Indy." I'm not sure if this relocation depending on how well she was doing was beneficial to anyone except the airlines, but we all got used to her not being at home.

As a psychology graduate from college, I understand the power of the mind's ability to suppress emotional pain. From experience, I know its power as my memory of the period of my mother's depression is confined to only the better aspects of my life. I distinctly remember every high school party, prom date, exam, friends etc., but the memory of whether my mother was in Indy at specific times or Philly is quite faded. I remember Christmas dances at my school, but I can't remember which Christmas we spent in Indy and which in Philly. Between my sophomore year of high school and sophomore year at college, it was a constant battle to maintain sanity and to deal with the issues at home.

In the fall of my sophomore year at college, my mother was doing a bit better, which, given the depths I had seen her in, meant merely getting out of bed and maybe getting changed. But this particular fall things seemed a little different, somehow she seemed to be coming back to us. The illness that had stolen her humor, sensitivity, and reality seemed to be returning what it had taken. My mother and oldest sister, Mary, visited me at school. We ate dinner and conversed in the car before I returned to the dorm. This was the last time I would see my mother alive. I look back now and wonder if she knew the end of her pain was near. About a month before her suicide she visited each one of us and was more stable than I had seen her in quite some time. I now can't help but think that this was no coincidence. I wonder if she had found a solution and a resolution to her pain and was feeling better in her "goodbye" to all of us.

On November 11, around eight in the morning, the phone rang. I had gotten in late the night before from an out-of-town football game. I was feeling some of the discomfort so many college students feel on a Sunday morning and decided not to answer the phone for fear it was the fraternity calling to enlist me for some work. But the answering machine clicked on and upon hearing my brother's voice I sprang to the phone. As I picked up the receiver I knew something was wrong. "Chris, this is Joe," I heard my seventeen-year-old brother say. "Dad came home from church and found Mom in the garage. I might as well come out and say it, um . . . Mom's dead." I repeated the last two words as tears and horror came over me. It seemed as though the whole world stopped and stood motionless for the next couple of minutes. I wanted to rush home, but I didn't have a car. Joe told me a family friend, whom I hardly knew, would be coming to get me. I wrote my roommate a note, "went home, will explain later," and was struck by the date as I wrote 11/11. I don't envy the stranger who got to take the kid whose mother had just committed suicide on an hour-long trip back to Indy; needless to say, we didn't have any great conversations, but I do remember what an incredibly beautiful fall day it was. The leaves were spectacular in color, and as Mother Nature was ending another season, I felt the end of something equally as powerful behind me.

At the wake, I remember being eerily calm. In many ways I found my mother's death a relief. She was no longer in pain, and we no longer had to see her suffer. Being physically present throughout my mother's illness, my father, brother, and I found more pain in her life and hence some relief in her death. For my sisters, who were at college and graduate school respectively, thus gone nine months of the year, it was her death that hurt the most.

The past seven years have been spent dealing, or not dealing, with my mother's death. Because my mother was absent so much in my later high school years, I became very independent, almost to a fault. With my mother gone, I was afraid to rely on anyone for fear that they might die or fail me in some other way. My then thirteen-year-old brother and I had to learn to take care of ourselves. And we did. We had a cleaning lady who kept up the house and a laundry woman who washed our clothes, but we suddenly needed to make doctor appointments, dinner, etc. I think my father tried to make the reality of an absent mother as easy as possible, often with money or other items of convenience, but there was no replacement for her presence.

I was twenty at the time my mother died, and dealing with her death while I was in college was far different than dealing with her life while I was in high school. Looking back, I realize that subconsciously I didn't want to follow in my mother's footsteps, who found life painful and miserable, so I adopted a reverse course and set out in search of only a good time. "You only live once, *carpe diem*" was my motto. Within the five years following my mother's death, my grandfather died of Alzheimer's, my favorite high school teacher died of unexpected heart failure, an aunt died of cancer, a high school friend contracted a rare bone disease and died, a college friend died of cancer, a high school friend was killed in an auto accident, another high school classmate was murdered. All these deaths reinforced my Ferris Bueller "Life moves fast, you better take a look around, you might miss it" attitude. At the rate things were going, I came to expect a death about once every three months and so was adamant about living life to the hilt. I somehow managed to maintain a dean's list grade point average, so no one knew that partying had taken precedence. I never advertised with long hair, tattoos, or body piercing that I was using drugs or drinking heavily and regularly. I kept my partying covert, but in college I wasn't that far from the norm, and as long as my grades were good, who'd notice?

I don't necessarily believe that I was hiding from the pain. Sure, some of my habits were self-medicating, but for the most part I wasn't running from something, but running to something. I only wanted to have fun and happiness. I believed for some time that if my only pursuit was happiness, I'd never end up like my mother. I didn't search for pleasure so much that I sacrificed the future, but living for the day certainly had become habit. It wasn't until a couple of years after college that my party scene began to slow down.

I moved to Atlanta, partly for a new adventure, but somewhat because I was ready to be away from the place that had so many memories of my home, my family, and particularly my mother. I also wanted to put the past behind me, start off new in a sense, but I also didn't want to be forever known as the kid whose mother committed suicide. I hate the fact that her death now overshadows her life. I wouldn't mind talking about it as much if I didn't feel the need to explain who she was before the onset of her depression. My mother was such a warm, intelligent, and sensitive person, but I feel her suicide distorts the person she really was. It's just too time consuming to give everyone the "full story," so I prefer not to go into it at all. When I am getting to know someone new, I often feel anxious about the inevitable question about my mother. I don't want my mother or me, to be tarred by the stigma of suicide. I feel much less embarrassed about her suicide with people who knew her, than with those who only know of her and whose thoughts will be dominated by the manner of her death. A friend put it perfectly in telling me that "my mother was too kind and intelligent for this world." Today, I still admire her strength for fighting so long.

I've tried to find meaning in my mother's death, but I have found none. I don't believe that God, or any other "force," had some deeper meaning in her suicide. I found both positive and negative results in my mother's death, but I don't buy the "it was meant to be, or God wanted her up there with Him" theory so many people tried to comfort me with. While I know everyone had good intentions and was sincere in their words of kindness to me, the best words came from a friend whose mother also committed suicide. Although his situation was much different than mine (his mother committed suicide after discovering her husband was having an affair), his words made more sense to me than anyone else's as he said, "It f—ing sucks!" Those blunt, yet profound words made more sense to me than any others. Perhaps our shared experience gave us a unique perspective, but I find much more comfort in those words than the "it was meant to happen" cop out.

I still fear that depression lurks in the shadows of my or one of my siblings' minds. I try to convince myself that this experience was a rite of passage and that I will become stronger because of it, and in some ways I have. But I also find that I'm more easily haunted by anxiety, and I wonder who the next shattering phone call will be about.

Christopher Stimming

Christopher Stimming was twenty in 1990 when his mother, aged fifty-seven, completed suicide.

What Life Has to Offer

[Our brother Joe turned seventeen one month before our mother killed herself. Although he misses by one year the definitional criteria we established for the adult child, perspectives on our mother's death would be incomplete without his inclusion. However, we remain convinced that his experience has been one more properly understood in terms of adolescent development. Hence, what follows is not a reflection on his more recent adult experience, but a college application essay he wrote when he was eighteen. In connection with his closing sentence, Joe comments now that although he still holds this conviction, the past seven years have proven this to be far more difficult than he had ever imagined. — EDS.]

The key to knowing me is to know about my mother. She became clinically depressed when I was thirteen and committed suicide in the late fall of my junior year. The interim years were filled with her treatment, both in and out of state. Needless to say, my mother and what happened to her are the most influential aspects of my life.

The Bible, specifically James, says to "consider it pure joy whenever you face trials of many kinds, because you know that the testing of your faith develops perseverance. Perseverance must finish its work so you may become mature and complete, lacking nothing." Obviously, I'd prefer being immature and incomplete in order to have my mom back. I didn't consider her illness "pure joy," either.

However, amidst all the frustration and pain, I became a better person. I matured at a young age and developed a greater sense of self-reliance. I also feel I am more sensitive to others who have experienced loss, and I am better able to help them. A few months after my mother's death, I was able to help a friend whose mother died of a heart attack. Although everyone deals with loss differently, I tried to tell her the things that helped me. But more important, instead of smothering her with advice, I became a sympathetic ear. And although my life thus far hasn't turned out how I wanted, I can say I'm a stronger person for it.

Another way to tell you about myself is to tell you how other people see me. In my junior year I was lead writer for our Junior Spectacular. Spectacular consists of four, twenty-minute acts written, directed, and performed by juniors as a fundraiser for the prom. As lead writer, with two assistants, I was the person in charge of our act.

It was difficult for me as well as for my friends for me to be put in an authoritative role. As the practices dragged on, tensions mounted. Even though I hoped it was in jest, the actors' union threatened to drown me in the YMCA pool. By the time we finished, however, the cast realized how much work the writers had put into it and how much we cared, not only about the production, but also about the people. I was quite proud when after the final performance, they gave me a Recognition Award.

I understand that in your directions you asked for an essay to let you know me. It may seem that I have written two entirely different ones. However, there is a very unique tie. In the Junior Spectacular play the thief Mickey is the spokesperson for "Life" cereal. He steals the prizes out of other cereal boxes claiming that "Life never has anything good to offer." But in the last spoken line another character says that "Mickey was wrong after all. I realize now, no matter what, life always has something good to offer." Ironically, this line comes from a boy whose mother killed herself. It's not that I'm an extreme optimist. My best and most dominating quality involves what was discussed in James earlier: Perseverance. I hope the worst times of my life are behind me. But I know I can handle any adversity life can offer. I will always plan on life having something good to offer, and I will not quit until I find it.

Joseph Stimming

Joseph Stimming was seventeen in 1990 when his mother, aged fifty-seven, completed suicide.

IV

Research and Resources

The Puzzle of Suicide in Late Life

The Paradox

Only 15 percent or so of all older adults who die by suicide have ever made any form of suicide attempt before in their lives. Is it possible that these suicide victims in their seventies, or eighties, or nineties, led charmed lives until relatively late in the age span—that they never before experienced the sort of "hard times" that might evoke a suicidal coping response from a vulnerable person? How is it possible to show suicidal behavior as a coping response for the first time at so late an age?

One popular explanation of this paradox is that older adulthood is accompanied by unique qualities of suffering, specifically one or more of the following: (a) global sadness and psychological impoverishment as a predominant characteristic of late life; (b) loneliness as a function of accumulating deaths of beloved family members, friends, and peers; (c) absence of meaningful work and productive activities; (d) restricted financial means or poverty; (e) disintegrating health; and (f) nearing specter of uncomfortable death. But is it true that these late-life stressors have a distinct quality that renders them more painful and more unbearable than the parallel stressors faced by younger adults? Is it true that many older adults laboring under the influence of these late-life stressors consider suicide? Is it true that these stressors are key factors (are they even present?) in most cases of older adult suicide?

A wide variety of clinical and research experiences contradicts the notion that the list of late-life stressors just itemized has much bearing on cases of suicide by elderly persons. Our work at the Center for Suicide Research and Prevention at the Rush-Presbyterian–St. Luke's Medical Center in Chicago has included outpatient and inpatient clinical work over several decades with older adults—including those who have suicidal thoughts and those who have made suicide attempts. We have intensively studied a large series of individual cases of older adult death by suicide in the community, with access to spouses, sons and daughters, and other relatives, as well as access to medical records and treating physicians. The portrait of suicide that emerges from psychotherapy with suicidal older adults and "psychological autopsy studies" of those who died by suicide converge to refute popular beliefs and assumptions.

A large and representative group of suicides by persons aged sixty-five years and over in the Chicago metropolitan area during one ten-month period showed many patterns characteristic of all suicides, regardless of age. Males predominated by a ratio of four to one. In terms of education and income, the older adults who died by suicide were representative of all older adults in the community at large—there was no excess of uneducated or poor, and no excess of highly educated or wealthy. (In this respect, suicide is unfortunately an "equal opportunity" tragedy.) Eighty-nine percent of the group were Caucasian.

With regard to their suicidal behavior, this series of elderly persons who died by suicide also showed patterns characteristic of all suicides. Fifty-three percent died using a firearm. Although 48 percent of the subjects were said to explicitly express thoughts of suicide in the last six months of life and another 26 percent repeatedly expressed thoughts of death, 89 percent of their next-of-kin whom we interviewed reported being surprised by the act of suicide. The first time the relatives ever identified these statements as clues to the impending suicide tended to be during the research interview weeks after the death.

The same group of suicides, however, violated many stereotypes that circulate about elderly suicide. Thirty-five percent of the subjects were married and living with their spouses at the time of death; only 35 percent were widowed. Seven percent had never been married. Fifty-six percent of the suicide victims were living with spouses or other family members at the time of their death. In this sample, no subjects were living in nursing homes or any other type of residential facility at the time of the suicide. Indeed, national data show that the suicide rate for institutionalized elderly persons is approximately half that of elderly persons living in the community. Overall, we had no difficulty identifying three or more family members—usually spouses, adult children, nieces, or nephews—or close friends per case willing to provide us with detailed information about the weeks preceding death (Younger, Clark, Ochmig-Lindberg, and Stein 1990).

Sixty percent of the subjects visited others outside the home weekly and 98 percent had weekly contact with friends and relatives; thus the vast majority of our subjects were not isolated from family and friends. Thirteen percent of the suicide victims were terminally ill, and another 24 percent had a severe chronic medical illness, but 63 percent were in relatively good health for persons in their seventies, eighties, or nineties. Stressful life events did not seem to characterize the older adult suicides as a group. Eleven percent faced the possibility of a change in their living situation (wanted or unwanted), 7 percent had experienced the death of a spouse within the last twelve months, and only 6 percent were having any kind of financial difficulties. So generally it is not fair to conclude that the elderly suicide victims were socially isolated or in poor health compared to other persons their age, or under more acute life stress than other persons their age.

If information about health and social circumstances do not help pinpoint which older adults die by suicide, if the most physically ill and the most socially crushed older adults are not the ones more prone to suicide, how are the suicides to be understood at all?

Actual suicides by adults aged sixty-five years and over fall into three broad categories. One category includes cases that closely parallel the mechanism of middle-aged suicide ("not distinctively elderly suicides"). The second category includes cases where the victim has been required to endure too many in a series of late-life embarrassments ("protest suicides"). The third category includes cases where the subject, responding to some inner prerecorded detailed script of exactly how death will progress from painful to intolerable, decides to leave life before reaching the intolerable portions of the script ("preemptive suicides").

Not Distinctively Elderly Suicides

Many suicides by persons in their seventies, eighties, and nineties seem no different than suicides by younger adults, and they seem to require no special developmental model or theory (thus, "not distinctively elderly suicides"). In all studies of completed suicide the world over, for all age groups, researchers have consistently found that 95 percent or more of all suicide victims were affected by a major psychiatric disorder, though that disorder went undetected and untreated in half or more of all cases. Detailed clinical interviews with the next-of-kin and close friends of the person who died by suicide, facilitating a comprehensive review of verbalizations and behaviors in the weeks leading up to death, have permitted researchers to pinpoint applicable symptoms and diagnoses, whether or not the illness had been recognized before. In approximately 60 percent of all cases of suicide—and 83 percent of elderly suicides—major depression plays a pivotal role in facilitating suicide. In approximately 20 percent of all cases of suicide, alcoholism or drug abuse (including abuse of prescribed drugs such as Xanax) plays a pivotal role.

National epidemiological studies of the incidence and prevalence of psychiatric disorders indicate that the elderly do not show higher rates of major depression than do middle-aged or young adults. Major depression should be considered an unusual, impairing, and treatable illness regardless of age. Sometimes "ageism," or the tendency to think that older adults are supposed to be depressed and that it is futile to treat their depression, discourages family members and friends from recognizing the gravity of a depressive illness in the aged. Sometimes the person's own tendency to misread the thoughts, feelings, and symptoms of depression as markers of interpersonal stress, physical illness, or general life problems cloud the affected person's own ability to recognize the gravity of a depressive illness. The loss of insight and the slowness to recognize a depressive disorder in oneself are common features of depressive illness and are most frequently encountered in two groups: (a) those who have not had the misfortune to weather an episode of depression ever before in their lives (some people have their first depression at age eighty-five); and (b) those who have not ever availed themselves of professional help for prior episodes of depression.

The inclination to believe that the depression is not "real" and not "inside," but is entirely the result of temporary problems caused by the real outside world, is common among family members and friends who have never experienced depression themselves, who find it hard to believe that their loved one (who has always been healthy and vital and free of depression) might now be crippled by depressive thoughts and contemplating suicide. The eminent suicidologist George Murphy has written about this trap which commonly misleads the layperson and the mental health professional. He notes that sometimes "A psychological explanation for the patient's emotional state appears to have served in lieu of diagnosis and treatment" (Murphy 1975, 307). Sometimes laypersons and mental health professionals alike try to "explain" the anguish and symptoms of a loved one by resorting to theories of how life events have conspired to overwhelm the affected person or how inner

150 David C. Clark

struggles have tied the affected person in knots—theories that sound authoritative and final, but which in truth distract everyone's attention from the simple recognition of the symptoms of a depressive illness or a suicidal crisis.

Alcohol and drug abuse are often overlooked as risk factors for elderly suicide. Many people overlook alcohol and drug misuse by other persons, even loved ones, preferring not to appear critical or judgmental. Another reason is that some believe the elderly have "earned" the right (by virtue of their long years) to misbehave in any way they please. A third reason is that alcohol and drug abuse are often subtle, bordering on the invisible; the affected person may conceal his or her substance use or may binge intermittently in the privacy of his or her own home. Finally, many family members assume (erroneously) that if a medication has been prescribed by a doctor, a layperson does not have the authority to raise questions about "overuse" or "misuse" of the prescribed drug.

Protest Suicides

In a previous paper, we unveiled the "Wedding Cake Model" of older adult suicide, which I think is more clearly referred to as "protest" suicide (Clark 1993). This idea, developed together with my colleague Susan Clark, had its beginnings in the observation that while the sorts of life events that seemed to trigger suicidal threats and suicidal behavior in some elderly persons appeared mundane, they no longer appeared so if we studied the person back over a period of years. With the help of a longer period of observation, we discovered that mundane events triggering suicidal behavior in the elderly often represented one too many in a series of "embarrassments," embarrassments that interacted with emerging major depression or preexisting alcohol or drug abuse disorder to yield a dangerous suicidal crisis.

We hypothesized that at some arbitrary point in the life span, the older adult begins to experience physical and psychological events that challenge the human tendency to think of the self as young, resilient, and indestructible. The point at which this experience begins, and the kinds of physical and psychological events that most directly challenge the person's belief system, vary from person to person. While most people hate to admit their human frailties, and most are dragged kicking and screaming into a gradual admission of their physical limitations, most are flexible enough to adjust. Eventually they acknowledge the undeniable facts of aging; they grieve for their youth, strength, or health; modify their self-identity to fit the new facts; and find new ways to realize their goals.

A small number of older adults, for reasons of long-standing personality, do not seem to have the flexibility to incorporate evidence of physical decline or to redefine themselves. For their entire adult lives, they were fiercely proud and independent. Their sense of self was defined in large part by their energy and productivity. They maintained an exaggerated Yankee sense of self-sufficiency. So when they begin to encounter evidence of their own physical decline, or evidence of a need to rely increasingly on others for help with routine activities, they are virtually incapable of bending and adjusting in the manner of most other older adults.

The small but disruptive encounters with evidence of physical or mental decline, or of the need to rely more on others, may be straightforward (clumsiness, inability to do a long-accustomed chore) or symbolic (a family member stripping him or her of the car keys). But these instances repeat and accumulate in number, with the annoying insistence of the sound of a leaky faucet in a cavernous tub. While these encounters (considered one at a time) are no different than those that thousands of older adults meet and adjust to every day, they strain and finally crack the stubborn immobility of the inflexible types.

Many of the intolerable encounters, or "cracks," are accompanied by a stream of angry denial ("of course I can do it!"), a refusal to let anyone else help, and suicidal talk or threats. We believe that these suicidal communications betray the nature of the underlying problem for the first time and signal the older adult's true sense that if the intolerable encounters continue, he or she is capable of suicide. The protest should be heeded; it is genuine and grave.

We do not believe that these types of inflexible persons progress into suicide unless one of the major psychiatric disorders kicks in (e.g., major depression) or has been simmering in the background for a long time (e.g., alcohol or drug abuse). Any of these three pernicious illnesses may heighten the sense of hopelessness, painful anxiety, already rigid thinking, over-sensitivity to physical feelings and symptoms, and dull judgment or insight in even the most intelligent and educated of older adults.

These acute symptom changes, combined with the anger, isolation, and despair already brewing as a reaction to the accumulation of intolerable encounters, makes for an extremely volatile potential for suicide. The proverbial "straw that breaks the camel's back" may be all that is required to overwhelm the person's ability to fend off the truth — that he or she is no longer as young, vital, and healthy as he or she needs to believe. This break-through facing-of-intolerable-facts may release flooding, overwhelming states of panic and rage, states that make suicide seem like "the sensible thing to do." Norman Mailer has written evocatively about this motive for suicide (the second in his list), where the real intent is to destroy the "termites, not the barn:"

> Suicide might be better understood on the assumption that there was not one reason for the act but two: People may kill themselves for the obvious reason, that they are washed up, spiritually humiliated down to zero; equally, they can see their suicide as an honorable termination of deep-seated terror. Some people . . . become so

mired in evil spirits that they believe they can destroy whole armies
of malignity by their own demise. It is like burning a barn to wipe
out the termites who might otherwise infest the house. (Mailer
1991, 12)

Preemptive Suicides

Finally, I want to highlight a small number of cases of elderly
death by suicide where the person developed an exaggerated sense
of déjà vu. While not accounting for a large portion of all elderly
suicides, these cases are generally men and women who have lived
through some harrowing experience of loss, the death of a spouse
or other close family member, and who were deeply impressed to
the point of terror by how intolerably the illness and the death unfolded. The painful experience and imprint may in some cases be
especially deep and indescribable because: (a) death occurred
when the subject was very young; (b) the relationship between the
two was extremely close, and the subject imagined feeling everything that the patient was going through; (c) the subject had little
information or knowledge about the illness and its course, so every
turn and change was unbearably frightening; or (d) the subject felt
that the patient counted on him or her to "do something," so much
so that the subject felt like a helpless failure in the situation.

In any case, those prone to preemptive suicide have a script
chiseled into their brain of how the original illness and death unfolded, and they have an unshakable conviction that when they
become severely ill, their own death will follow the exact same
script. While some of their fears may have merit (they are not irrational), the important point is that their anxiety is rooted in their
memory, and their anxiety tends to guide all their decisions. If one
interviews them carefully about the nature of their illness and how
they expect their illness to play out, the fact that they are paying
little or no attention to the facts of their own case and situation be-

comes immediately obvious. If one tests their ability to change their thinking depending on the diagnosis, the course of their illness, and their response to different treatment interventions, one finds that they cannot assimilate the here-and-now information. They are stuck making decisions for themselves based on a scenario that unfolded years or even decades ago, around another patient and another illness.

Furthermore, older adults do not have to be very ill at all to be susceptible to preemptive suicide. Sometimes a depressed person's preoccupation with physical symptoms—e.g., aches and pains, flu, or physical symptoms of depression—becomes so intense that he or she makes the mistake of jumping to the conclusion that he or she is dying (for example, of cancer), despite contrary medical evidence and opinion. At this point many depressed patients may avoid all further contact with physicians, preferring to be "left alone to die." In two community-based studies of elderly persons who died by suicide, there were more persons who killed themselves because they mistakenly believed they had cancer than there were persons who died with cancer or any other terminal illness (Conwell, Caine, and Olsen 1990; Murphy 1977).

Conclusions

Suicide comes as a fright and a shock, wherever and whenever it occurs. It typically catches a family by complete surprise, even if afterward it is not hard to ascertain that the victim had been voicing morbid or suicidal ideas in the weeks leading up to his or her death, and that the victim had been troubled by a variety of symptoms and impairments that (retrospectively) amount to a psychiatric disorder. Remember that in the physician's office, clinical studies show that general practitioners fail to recognize about half the cases of patients who appear for physical symptoms but (unknowingly) qualify for a diagnosis of major depression.

While the hope is that general practitioners and family members alike will become more knowledgeable about major depression and become more skilled at recognizing the related suicide risk, the bottom line is that major depression is not simple to detect and diagnose, even for the professional. The family member may have a strong disadvantage when compared to the general practitioner, as well—there is some evidence that knowledgeable and skilled family members have an emotional blind spot that makes it particularly difficult to recognize psychiatric symptoms and suicidal communications in a loved one. Perhaps the symptoms and suicidal impulses are sometimes too painful and threatening to face, despite our eagerness to help and protect the individual. If major psychiatric disorder contributes in profound ways to suicidal thinking and suicidal behavior, what can family members do to help—beyond being alert to the possibility of psychiatric disorder, helping the loved one get good professional treatment, and pushing the loved one to stay compliant with the treatment plan? There is much they can do, and the part they can play was said best by Esquirol, one of the leading nineteenth-century psychiatrists:

> Neither argument nor sympathy, individually or united, ever yet cured a case of suicidal insanity, or ever caused a patient to fully appreciate the considerations offered for his relief, however well suited to his condition; yet the fact, that they furnish evidence that he is not quite forgotten, and that his friends do not regard his state as altogether hopeless, lessens for a brief space, the overwhelming burden which rests upon his mind. The daily expressions of sympathy and hope, in connection with the assiduous attentions of devoted and affectionate attendants, doubtless give to the agents of a medicinal character which may be employed, a degree of efficacy which they would not otherwise manifest. (Esquirol [1845] 1965)

David C. Clark, Ph.D.
Stanley G. Harris Family Professor of Psychiatry, Rush Medical College
Director, Center for Suicide Research and Prevention
Rush-Presbyterian–St. Luke's Medical Center, Chicago

References

Clark, D. C. 1993. Narcissistic crises of aging and suicidal despair. *Suicide and Life-Threatening Behavior* 23:21–26.

Conwell, Y., Caine, E. D., and Olsen, K. 1990. Suicide and cancer in late life. *Hospital and Community Psychiatry* 41: 1334–1339.

Esquirol, J.E.D. [1845]. 1965. *Mental Maladies: A Treatise on Insanity.* Facsimile edition, Library of the New York Academy of Medicine. New York: Hafner Publishing Company.

Mailer, Norman. 1991. *Harlot's Ghost.*

Murphy, G. E. 1975. The physician's responsibility for suicide. II. Errors of omission. *Annals of Internal Medicine* 82: 305–309.

Murphy, G. E. 1977. Cancer and the coroner. *Journal of the American Medical Association* 237: 786–788.

Younger, S. C., Clark, D. C., Oehmig-Lindroth, R., Stein, R. J. 1990. Availability of knowledgeable informants for a psychological autopsy study of suicides committed by elderly persons. *Journal of the American Geriatrics Society* 38:1169–1175.

Research on Survivors of Suicide

A shared primary goal of suicide researchers, therapists, support group leaders and facilitators, and survivors is to understand suicide bereavement, including its commonalities and individual differences. Sound research investigations are needed to obtain the support and allocation of resources in the larger health community that are necessary to provide such understanding and to assist in healing. Early research investigations on survivors of suicide had a number of undesirable methodological problems that limited their ability to be accepted or to fully portray suicide survivorship (see e.g., Calhoun, Selby, and Selby 1982). These studies were important, however, in describing some of the varied aspects of suicide survivor grief.

The most important reason that these early investigations could not answer questions about how suicide grief was different from bereavement associated with other modes of death was that the research did not include comparison groups. Only suicide survivors were studied. When Calhoun et al. (1982) reviewed the existing research literature on suicide survivorship, they found that not a single one included a comparison group. To understand how two types of grief differ, it is necessary to study both with the same methods, procedures, and measures. Despite the lack of comparison groups, these studies had their place in the development of knowledge about survivors of suicide experiences. These studies represent the exploratory stages of research in which descriptive goals are met; they have helped us to recognize some of the variability as well as probable common aspects of suicide survivorship. Some of the findings of these studies will be described below in the context of the larger research literature.

Before proceeding to a consideration of the results of research, however, some comments are warranted regarding the place and role of personal accounts in the context of our knowledge about suicide survivorship. As will be seen, although research is highly desirable as an information-gathering technique, there is a clear and important role for the individual perspective as well.

Suicide Survivors Literature: Personal Accounts

A natural question that arises with the accumulating research evidence on survivors of suicide surrounds the need for individual accounts, experiences, and "stories." The existence of research investigations and their findings does not diminish the continuing importance or need for such personal accounts. Research studies attempt to show "average" or "typical" reactions, they portray predominantly group results, masking or hiding the individual cases that comprise the group. The range of responses and the rich detail and complexity of individual experiences are necessarily lost in the description of such findings. With research studies we obtain an emphasis on the general aspects of grief and bereavement; individual accounts reveal detailed experience, thoughts, and actions of the single person. Personal accounts help us to empathize with the person as an individual, to see the continuity of thoughts and feelings as well as their continuities and discontinuities over time. They also help other survivors to normalize feelings they might have, to understand that they are not alone in this experience and its complexity of thoughts, feelings, and behaviors.

Still largely lacking among these individual accounts are clinical case studies of those with difficult or problematic grief. The majority of the existing literature in this area tends to be among those who most certainly experienced difficulties with their bereavement process, but rarely if ever could their grief be considered "pathological." Since most individuals who lose a loved one to suicide seem to fall in this latter category, they are crucial to our total body of knowledge and information. However, the clinical literature needs cases across the entire range of experience to inform therapy as well as supportive interventions.

Within the "personal accounts" literature, there has been a highly desirable progression. Among the first of these accounts were often those of either mothers, such as Iris Bolton's *My Son, My Son* (1983); Wrobleski's account as a stepmother (1994), or wives, such as Betsy Ross (1996, 1997). Since that time other relationships have appeared in the literature that have begun to provide an increasingly more complete picture of the variety of survivor experiences. These more recent accounts include those of children, e.g., Mariette Hartley's revelations about her father's suicide (1990), siblings (Hebert 1987, 95–103), adult child survivors (such as the present work), and even men's experiences as widowers (Clarke 1989; Organ 1979) and fathers (Bolton, I. 1983, 1987). See Table 1 for a partial listing of these relationships and publications in which these personal accounts may be found. There remain a number of relationships not yet shared in the literature (e.g., grandparents, family survivors of elderly suicides other than spouses, close friends and confidants, etc.), but the expanding literature in this area, mostly for relationships portrayed also by others (mothers, wives, etc., see Table 1 for specific references) have each added the rich, great variety that is unique to survivor experiences along with the number of commonalities. Far less common has been the survivor accounts of what therapy and support group experiences were like for them and how these approaches seemed to have benefited them. Ross's description of the Ray of Hope program she developed in the late 1970s in response to her husband's suicide remains one of the few highly detailed program descriptions. (See also Rogers, Sheldon, Barwick, Letofsky, and Lancee 1982; Rubey 1985; Wrobleski 1984–85). However, it would also be valuable for survivors to discuss in detail their experiences

Table 1

Detailed Personal Accounts* of Suicide in the Literature, by Relationship to the Deceased

Mother of the suicide: Aarons (1995); Bolton, I.† (1983, 1984a, 1984b, 1986, 1987); Carlson (1995); Chance† (1988, 1992); Harness-Overly (1992); Hoffman (1987); "Joan" (in Alexander 1991); Langford (1989); White-Bowden (1985)

Stepmother of the suicide: Wrobleski (1994)

Father of the suicide: Bolton, J.† (Bolton, I. 1987)

Wife of the suicide: Fine (1997); "Laura" (in Alexander 1991); "Marcia" (in Alexander 1991); Moon (1986); Pesaresi (1987); Rivers (in Cullen 1988; 1991; 1997); Ross (1990; 1997)

Husband of the suicide: Clarke (1989); Organ (1979)

Children of the suicide: Anderson (1991; was 12 years old at the time of the death); "Cathy" (in Hurley 1991; was 4 1/2 years old at the time of the death); Hopkins (in Krementz 1981; was 7 years old at the time of the death); Joseph (in Krementz 1981; was 6 years old at the time of the death); "Joy" (in Alexander 1991; was 19 years old at the time of the death); "Karen" (in Alexander 1991; was 11 years old at the time of the death); Lockridge (1995; was 5 years old at the time of the death)

Adult Children of the suicide: Alexander (1987, 1991); Hartley (and Commire 1990); "Natalie" (in Alexander 1991); "Susan and Philip" (in Alexander 1991)

Sibling of the suicide: "Chris" (in Alexander 1991); Hebert (1987); Rhoda (in Buksbazen, 1976)

Lover/Partner of the suicide: "Catherine" (in Alexander 1991); "Richard" (in Alexander 1991)

Close Friend/Confidant of the suicide: "Rachel" (in Alexander 1991)

Classmates of the suicide: Bostwick (1987, medical students)

Therapist of the suicide: "Ellen" (in Alexander 1991); Foster (1987); Gorkin, (1985); Heilig, (1983); Jones (1987)

*The portrayals in Alexander (1991) are not exactly "personal accounts" since they are not written directly by the survivors themselves (although their quoted words are sometimes used). They are written by Alexander following her extensive interviews with the survivors. At the same time, these are not really "case studies" like others in the literature (e.g., Ballenger 1978; Berman 1990a, 1990b; Dalke 1994; Graves 1978; Horowitz and Hammer 1976; Ilan, 1973; Jakab and Howard 1969; Silverman 1972), which are typically written by a mental health professional in the context of a therapeutic intervention circumstance. Those appearing in Alexander, a survivor herself, are more similar to personal accounts than case studies in this author's opinion, and for that reason they have been included here.

†These survivors are mental health professionals who have experienced the loss through suicide of a family member.

from therapy or support groups, particularly to portray the progression, changes, frustrations, lessons learned, and stages of healing that likely resulted over time. It would also be important to study those who have problematic bereavement experiences to determine possible high-risk factors (e.g., age, social support available, those who find the body after the death, those who witness the actual act of the suicide, etc.). Findings might also demonstrate that potential early intervention might lessen those problems or assist in coping.

As a final comment and observation on the entire research and personal experience literature, there still seems to be an attempt or need to demonstrate that suicide grief is worse than that for other causes of death. Although I understand the need to identify the issues and demonstrate the importance of grief, is it not enough to show that suicide produces a different set of bereavement issues and patterns than for some causes but shares some similarities to others? As does everyone else I know in this area, I believe there are differences between suicide survivorship and that from other causes. Suicide complicates bereavement patterns, but the level and details of its uniqueness are not yet well established. Each group probably feels that its own pain is worse than that of others. Such a demonstration of greater severity or pain seems counterproductive and unnecessary to demonstrate the importance of this topic and the need for study and attention. Greatly expanded attention is needed to all types of grief and bereavement.

Survivors Research Findings: Early Non–Comparison Group Literature

While personal accounts are often a starting point in our gathering of information, the next logical progression is to research investigations. What appears to be the first comprehensive compilation and review of the existing seminal literature appeared in

Cain's introduction to his classic 1972 edited book *Survivors of Suicide*. In his "clustered and capsuled" portrayal he noted nine reactions and some brief elaborations of what Dunne (1987, 143) would later call the "survivor syndrome" (see also Dunne and Wilbur 1993). Reflecting particularly some of the psychodynamic considerations that he compiled, Cain (1972, 13–14) summarized these reactions as:

- reality distortion,
- guilt,
- impotent rage,
- identification with the suicide,
- incomplete mourning.
- tortured object-relations,
- disturbed self-concept,
- search for meaning,
- depression and self-destructiveness,

Even in this early consideration of a scant literature, Cain also noted in his comments behaviors such as

- anniversary reactions associated with the death,
- preoccupation with the phenomenon of suicide and involvement with prevention efforts, and
- feelings of shame, stigma, and abandonment.

The literature in the decade to follow, as reviewed by Calhoun et al. (1982) actually added little to this list, although the increase in the number of empirical studies was important to reinforce and highlight the set of reactions. (Two recent noncomparative studies likewise reveal little new to the reactions noted elsewhere; Grossman, Clark, Gross, Halstead, and Pennington 1995; Van Dongen, 1993).

Calhoun et al.'s review of the literature up to the early 1980s found an expanded literature, with verification for many of the reactions that Cain (1972) noted and an even longer list of possible additions to the survivor syndrome. Without comparison groups it was not possible to make any definitive statements regarding how suicide survivors and their survivor syndrome might differ or be similar to the grief and bereavement observed among survivors of other modes of death. However, Calhoun et al. expanded the reactions of Cain's list to include several categories and a number of new reactions. They organized the findings into affective (i.e., emotional), cognitive, behavioral, physical, and family interaction reactions. In most cases, a number of studies observed these reactions among suicide survivors. These additional reactions included

- relief,
- shock and disbelief,
- health-related problems as well as more physician visits and even higher mortality rates, and
- possible negative effects on the family system.

Perhaps most interesting about the review, Calhoun et al. admitted their inability to draw clear conclusions and generalizations about the unique aspects of suicide survivorship, but at the same time they attempted to derive a list of reactions that they believed might eventually be found to fit this uniqueness. Noting the great limitations in the research, Calhoun et al. suggested that there was enough consistency in the results to support only three cautious generalizations. That is, suicide survivors may be unique in their

- "search for an understanding of the death,"
- their greater feelings of guilt, and
- "the lower levels of social support" they are likely to receive (Calhoun, 1982, 417).

Thus, although both Cain and Calhoun et al. derived long lists of reactions associated with a possible suicide survivor syndrome, the evidence to support the majority of these list items as unique aspects of suicide survivor grief was lacking. That is not to say, however, that these reactions are not part of grief following suicide; it simply argues that research verification is lacking to support their uniqueness to suicide bereavement. In 1982, Calhoun et al. concluded that the extent to which suicide bereavement is different from that associated with other modes of death was unclear and perhaps limited to only a small subset of reactions.

Another interpretation of these findings might suggest that a larger set of reactions may be unique to the aftermath of suicide, not in their appearance alone, but perhaps in the quality of their appearance. That is, a reaction that is labeled the same by suicide survivors and those from other causes who are interviewed may indeed occur for both, but there may be facets and issues associated with that reaction that are unique to bereavement from one cause as compared to another. For example, suicide survivors and accident survivors may both feel some degree of guilt for actions they performed or those they might not have performed that they associate with some degree of responsibility for the death of their loved one. However, the amount and subjective aspects of guilt may differ generally for suicide as opposed to accident survivors. Thus far, research to address this kind of question is virtually nonexistent even in the comparative literature, and, of course, their determination is not possible in studies that only include survivors of one mode of death. A critical need exists for research that focuses on such a teasing out of specific bereavement reactions, both from a quantitative as well as qualitative viewpoint.

Survivors Research Findings: Comparison Group Literature

Subsequent to these first, exploratory investigations, a few noncomparative studies have been published as noted (i.e., Grossman et al. 1995, group of parents who survived child suicides; Van Dongen 1993, combined group of several relationships), and a number of other studies with stronger methodological qualities have been conducted. Compared to the total lack of comparison group studies observed by Calhoun and colleagues in 1982, McIntosh (1993) only a decade later reviewed fourteen published studies that included such groups. Since that time, an additional sixteen investigations have appeared in the published literature, with the largest number studying nonfamilial survivors (six studies of friends and peers of high school students: Brent, Moritz, Bridge, Perper, and Canobbio 1996a; Brent, Perper, Moritz, Allman, Liotus, Schweers, Roth, Balach, and Canobbio 1993; Brent, Perper, Moritz, Allman, Schweers, Roth, Balach, Canobbio, and Liotus 1993; Brent, Perper, Moritz, Friend, Schweers, Allman, McQuiston, Boylan, Roth, and Balach 1993; Brent, Perper, Moritz, Liotus, Richardson, Canobbio, Schweers, and Roth 1995; Brent, Perper, Moritz, Liotus, Schweers, and Canobbio 1994), as well as new studies of spouses (Cleiren, Grad, Zavasnik, and Diekstra 1996; Grad and Zavasnik 1996), parents (Séguin, Lesage, and Kiely 1995), siblings (an additional study by Brent and colleagues: Brent, Perper, Moritz, Liotus, Schweers, Roth, Balach, and Allman 1993), three studies of both parent and sibling survivors as a combined group (Brent, Moritz, Bridge, Perper, and Canobbio 1996b; Nelson and Frantz 1996; Pfeffer et al. 1997), and several studies of familial survivors combined as a single comparison group (Cleiren, Diekstra, Kerkhof, and van der Wal 1994; Reed 1993; Silverman, Range, and Overholser 1994–95; Thompson and Range 1992–93). This body of now thirty studies included the comparison groups of survivors of other modes of death that early suicide survivor studies lacked and improved other study aspects such as measurement of grief as well. Although not without their own limitations, the major advantage of these direct comparisons of survivors from two or more modes of death over the early exploratory investigations has been their ability to discover the differences as well as the similarities in grief associated with suicide, accidental, and natural deaths (and occasionally homicide as well).

The majority of these investigations have studied survivors of only one relationship category to the suicides they survive (i.e., parents only, widows only, etc.). This tendency has existed for some time, in apparent recognition that each type of relationship seems to involve its own aspects of grief and bereavement, and thus the study of survivors by specific relationships seems to hold the most potential for revealing useful findings and promise of enhancing our knowledge and understanding. Although all survivors will likely experience many of the reactions noted in the early research above to varying degrees, the kinship relation of the individual may attenuate or alter the reactions and the specific set that is experienced. At the same time, few individual survivors will likely experience the entire set of reactions or necessarily experience them to the same degree as another survivor. The research on relationships has been reviewed in detail previously (e.g., McIntosh 1987b, 1993). Therefore, only the most salient results will be outlined here, particularly since no research exists regarding adult survivors of parental suicide.

In a general sense, a number of overall findings from this body of literature can largely be summarized as McIntosh (1993) did. None of the investigations are without criticisms methodologically, but their collective results suggest six points. First, evidence supports a generally nonpathological bereavement reaction to suicide. Second, more similarities than differences are observed between suicide survivors and those from other modes of death, particularly when comparing suicide survivors to accidental death survivors. Third, possibly a small number of grief reactions or aspects of grieving may differ, or are unique, for suicide survivors (and these unique reactions along with the larger number may constitute a nonpathological but definable "survivor syndrome"), but the precise differences and unique characteristics are not yet fully apparent. Fourth, the course of suicide survivorship may differ from that of other survivors over time, but, fifth, by some time after the second year, differences in grief seem minimal or indistinguishable across survivor groups. Sixth, the kinship relation of the survivor to the suicide along with the precise closeness and quality of the relationship and the time that has passed since the suicide seem to be important factors in bereavement.

Beyond these general summary findings, specific results have also emerged. Due to the previous lack of comparative findings, the studies have often attempted to verify or refute the findings suggested by the noncomparative studies reviewed by Calhoun et al. (1982) or suggestions by Cain (1972). As might be expected, some aspects of grief have been shown to differ for suicide survivors compared to survivors of deaths by other means while findings for other reactions have not been differentially observed for suicide survivors. In addition, these results have not necessarily been consistent across studies with survivors of the same kinship relations nor across kinship relations. Because this book focuses on familial relationships, this brief review will omit the proportionately large number of studies of close friends and peers. Unfortunately, many of the studies of multiple relationships combined into a single group combine familial with nonfamilial survivors and are therefore also difficult to interpret in this regard. These studies will also be largely omitted here in favor of those investigations focused on specific familial kinship relations.

Parents surviving a child's suicide. Although present in studies of nearly all relationships, guilt and its related dimensions (such as shame and stigma) are perhaps the most prominent aspects of grief indicated among parents who have lost a child to suicide. The literature on attitudes toward parents of suicide victims underscore the belief that parents are blamed and held responsible for their child's death and they are liked less than parents whose child died by other means (e.g., Rudestam 1987). Although not all of the few studies of parents have found consistent results for these reactions when comparing this group to parent survivors of other modes of death, present findings often support this difference. Similarly, lack of support from others is prevalent in the accounts of parents, but research findings with comparative groups are either equivocal on this aspect or it has not been included in those grief aspects studied. Perhaps the results of Thompson and Range (1992–93), not a study of parents, is relevant here. They found greater variability in social support reported by suicide survivors compared to other survivors. This may account for some of the equivocality in these studies of parents. Finally, as in all modalities of death, both positive and negative outcomes in family adaptation occur, although parents surviving a suicide may more often experience negative adaptation (e.g., Séguin et al. 1995).

Spouse survivors. Nearly all studies of spouse survivors are of widows; that is, wives whose husbands committed suicide. This factor undoubtedly reflects the much higher levels of suicide by men and perhaps also the greater likelihood that women will more often agree to participate in research. Both early (McIntosh 1987b) and recent (Cleiren, Grad, et al. 1996; Grad and Zavasnik 1996) comparative studies have frequently found more similarities than differences for spouses of suicide and of accidental deaths. Specific study results have found differences between spouses who survive suicide as opposed to other modes of death, but there has not been much consistency in the particular aspects of grief for which differences are observed. That is, some studies find differences that are not observed in other investigations. Differences occur in aspects such as guilt, shame, stigma, and social support following the death. One important factor in the bereavement outcome may be the nature and quality of the marital relationship at the time of the spouse's suicide.

Children who survive the suicide of a parent. Although the issue of the age of the survivor (as well as the suicide) has frequently been noted in survivor studies, it is a particularly salient issue when children survive the suicide of a parent (but is also obviously important when the suicide was a sibling or other family member). It should be noted that the vast majority of studies of child survivors have studied children who are mental health clients, and this aspect may confound to some degree the findings reported. Particularly, the vulnerability and high risk of children for mental health symptoms is commonly observed (e.g., Pfeffer et al. 1997). Among the other aspects of grief that emerge in description of child survivors of parental suicide are the issues of guilt that children feel, the identification of the child with the deceased parent, and distortions and often misleading information provided to children by other family members. It should be reemphasized here that studies of adult children who survive the suicide of a parent have thus far not been conducted (or at least published).

Sibling survivors. The few studies of siblings that have appeared are again focused on psychopathology (Brent, Moritz, Bridge, Perper, and Canobbio 1996b; Brent, Perper, Moritz, Liotus, Schweers, Roth, Balach, and Allman 1993), and they show mixed results on the vulnerability of sibling survivors to psychiatric illness and symptoms following the suicide when compared to controls. One difference, however, was a longer period of higher grief symptoms among those who survived the suicide of an adolescent sibling. As in all other kinship relations, many more studies are needed of siblings before definitive conclusions can be drawn.

Suicide survivors research: Other methodological issues

Problems that exist in conducting survivors research, as well as difficulties with the research on survivors, have been detailed and known for some time (e.g., Cain 1972; Calhoun et al. 1982; Henslin

1971; McIntosh 1987a). Although the present chapter is not intended to detail these numerous problems, the general research issues that need to be addressed to improve future investigations include the need for replication of findings, the use of better sampling methods and larger numbers of survivors, development of better measures of general and specific aspects of bereavement, specific study of the entire range of kinship relations (both familial and others, including therapists), inclusions of measures of the emotional closeness or even the strength of the bond or attachment between the survivor and the person committing suicide, and the use of longitudinal research methods to determine the time course of bereavement. Future studies could also benefit from program evaluation studies and published descriptions of the programs (including all approaches: therapy, support group, self-help groups, etc.), studies of the effects of suicide on systems (e.g., family units, schools as a system, therapy groups, etc.), and the inclusion of nonbereaved control groups whenever possible. Perhaps obviously, comparative investigations that include several modes of death are generally preferable to noncomparative designs and will usually provide results that are more directly interpretable.

Research on Survivors: Epidemiological Issues
and Therapy Studies

One of the glaring omissions in the suicide survivor literature is the existence of a quality, well-conducted epidemiological study. This may seem unimportant, but as with all issues, the quantifiability of a problem or topic often determines the attention it receives and the amount of resources, including funds, allocated to studying the problem and to prevention efforts. This determination of the extent to which suicide survivorship is a mental health issue deserving of focused attention and support includes clarity with respect to any possible unique survivor syndrome as well as the number of individuals involved and even the "cost" of the behavior to society and individuals.

Although to this time no national or other epidemiological investigation has been conducted to clarify the probable number of individuals (and their characteristics, relationship to deceased, etc.) who have been affected by the suicide of a loved one, McIntosh (1989) advanced estimates of the number of survivors in the United States population, a basic and essential fact that must be determined if proper levels of attention and assistance are to be provided for survivors. Using these conservative figures, an estimated one of every fifty-nine Americans is a survivor of suicide, a conservative total of 4.43 million in 1995 (McIntosh 1997). If there are six survivors on the average for each suicide (Shneidman 1969), the 31,000 annual suicides produce an estimated 186,000 survivors each year, or a pace of six survivors every seventeen minutes (on average, there is a suicide every seventeen minutes), more than five hundred per day. Others (e.g., Callahan 1989) have suggested the number is higher, but without a quality epidemiological investigation, the estimate above will suffice ("Interaction" 1996).

A final issue of the survivors research literature is the relative sparsity of studies that investigate the efficacy of therapeutic and support interventions and programs. Notable exceptions to this omission include an evaluation study of the Los Angeles Suicide Prevention Center program (Farberow 1992) and a recent comparison of two bereavement group approaches (Constantino and Bricker 1996). Another interesting study (Hopmeyer and Werk 1994) compared peer support groups for suicide survivors with those for widows and relatives of those who died by cancer. Their results validate the benefits of support groups for all three survivor groups, while at the same time allowing the elaboration of differences as well as similarities in the experiences of the different survivor groups. Finally, Murphy (1996) describes an intervention program for parents who lost an adolescent to violent death. The authors then (Murphy et al. 1996) present the parents' perceptions of the support program. This literature is far too small to draw definitive conclusions, particularly in light of our lack of clear knowledge about the full range of programs and therapeutic approaches that exist (see Rubey and McIntosh 1996) and the general failure to design programs with crucial and essential ongoing evaluation components. In this same regard, it would be useful for survivors, therapists, and facilitators to describe the features of their group approach that have been perceived as most helpful as well as those components that did not seem to work as well, either generally and/or for specific subgroups of survivors.

Conclusion

The research literature continues to grow annually (see e.g., McIntosh 1985–86, 1996), including more and better designed studies that help us to quantify and place suicide grief in the larger context of bereavement from all modes of death. There is certainly a need for further expansion of this improving body of information, including studies of grief and bereavement among kinship groups thus far not systematically studied, which would include adult child survivors. This expanding knowledge of group findings also continues to be supplemented by the highly detailed individual accounts that both personalize suicide grief as well as portray the wide range of experiences in a way not possible in group research finding reports. The present literature has done much to raise awareness of this important aspect of suicidal behavior and establish therapy and support interventions, but more work remains to improve further the experience of survivors and especially to fill in the many details that are not yet known in the larger context of loss and grieving. Each of these areas deserves even more attention to increase our understanding, but more important, to assist attempts to help survivors confront and heal from their loss.

John L. McIntosh, Ph.D.
Professor of Psychology
Indiana University–South Bend

This chapter is dedicated to the memory of Adina Wrobleski, who passed away in the past year. Adina, the survivor of a stepchild's suicide, was an early survivor who spoke and wrote about survivors' issues, bringing attention to the topic both among the public and professional groups such as the American Association of Suicidology. Her efforts, particularly in the Minneapolis–St. Paul area where she lived, were of significant help to survivors and the survivor movement in general. Adina was the first survivor I met and, in addition to her friendship, she had a substantial impact on my initial awareness of and later study of survivors of suicide.

References

Aarons, L. 1995. *Prayers for Bobby: A mother's coming to terms with the suicide of her gay son.* San Francisco: Harper.

Alexander, V. 1987. Living through my mother's suicide. In *Suicide and its aftermath: Understanding and counseling the survivors,* edited by E. J. Dunne, J. L. McIntosh and K. L. Dunne-Maxim. 109–17. New York: Norton.

Alexander, V. 1991. *Words I never thought to speak: Stories of life in the wake of suicide.* New York: Lexington Books.

Anderson, D. B. 1991. Never too late: Resolving the grief of suicide. *Journal of Psychosocial Nursing* 29 no. 3: 29–31.

Ballenger, J. C. 1978. Patients' reactions to the suicide of their psychiatrist. *Journal of Nervous and Mental Disease* 166: 859–67.

Berman, A. L. 1990a. Case consultation: Suicide postvention. *Suicide and Life-Threatening Behavior* 20: 187–188. [2 case vignettes; 12-year-old and

13-year-old] [Carter, B. F., and A. Brooks. Comment. 188–90. Peck, M. L. Comment. 191–92.]

Berman, A. L. 1990b. Case consultation: The Miltons [parent survivors of a child suicide]. *Suicide and Life-Threatening Behavior* 20: 364–66. [1 case vignette] [Dunne, E. J. Comment. 367–69. Messersmith, C. E. Comment. 369–72.]

Bolton, I., with C. Mitchell. 1983. *My son, my son: A guide to healing after a suicide in the family.* Atlanta: Bolton Press.

Bolton, I. 1984a. A mother's personal experience in the loss of a son through suicide. In *Suicide: The will to live vs. the will to die,* edited by N. Linzer. 187–207. New York: Human Sciences Press.

Bolton, I. 1984b. Families coping with suicide. In *Death and grief in the family,* edited by T. T. Frantz. 35–47. Rockville, MD: Aspen.

Bolton, I. 1986. Death of a child by suicide. In *Parental loss of a child,* edited by T. A. Rando. 201–12. Champaign, IL: Research Press Company.

Bolton, I. 1987. Our son Mitch. In *Suicide and its aftermath: Understanding and counseling the survivors,* edited by E. J. Dunne, J. L. McIntosh and K. L. Dunne-Maxim. 85–94. New York: Norton.

Bostwick, M. 1987. After a suicide. *The New Physician,* July–August 15–17.

Brent, D. A., G. Moritz, J. Bridge, J. Perper, and R. Canobbio. 1996a. Long-term impact of exposure to suicide: A three-year controlled follow-up. *Journal of the American Academy of Child and Adolescent Psychiatry* 35: 646–53.

Brent, D. A., G. Moritz, J. Bridge, J. Perper, and R. Canobbio. 1996b. The impact of adolescent suicide on siblings and parents: A longitudinal follow-up. *Suicide and Life-Threatening Behavior* 26: 253–59.

Brent, D. A., J. Perper, G. Moritz, C. Allman, L. Liotus, J. Schweers, C. Roth, L. Balach, and R. Canobbio. 1993. Bereavement or depression? The impact of the loss of a friend to suicide. *Journal of the American Academy of Child and Adolescent Psychiatry* 32: 1189–97.

Brent, D. A., J. A. Perper, G. Moritz, C. Allman, J. Schweers, C. Roth, L. Balach, R. Canobbio, and L. Liotus. 1993. Psychiatric sequelae to the loss of an adolescent peer to suicide. *Journal of the American Academy of Child and Adolescent Psychiatry* 32: 509–17.

Brent, D. A., J. Perper, G. Moritz, A. Friend, J. Schweers, C. Allman, L. McQuiston, M. B. Boylan, C. Roth, and L. Balach. 1993. Adolescent witnesses to a peer suicide. *Journal of the American Academy of Child and Adolescent Psychiatry* 32: 1184–88.

Brent, D. A., J. A. Perper, G. Moritz, L. Liotus, D. Richardson, R. Canobbio, J. Schweers, and C. Roth. 1995. Posttraumatic stress disorder in peers of adolescent suicide victims: Predisposing factors and phenomenology. *Journal of the American Academy of Child and Adolescent Psychiatry* 34: 209–15.

Brent, D. A., J. A. Perper, G. Moritz, L. Liotus, J. Schweers, and R. Canobbio. 1994. Major depression or uncomplicated bereavement? A follow-up of youth exposed to suicide. *Journal of the American Academy of Child and Adolescent Psychiatry* 33: 231–39.

Brent, D. A., J. A. Perper, G. Moritz, L. Liotus, J. Schweers, C. Roth, L. Balach, and C. Allman. 1993. Psychiatric impact of the loss of an adolescent sibling to suicide. *Journal of Affective Disorders* 28: 249–56.

Buksbazen, C. 1976. Legacy of suicide. *Suicide and Life-Threatening Behavior* 6: 106–22.

Cain, A. C., ed. 1972. *Survivors of suicide.* Springfield, IL: Charles C. Thomas.

Calhoun, L. G., J. W. Selby, and L. E. Selby. 1982. The psychological aftermath of suicide: An analysis of current evidence. *Clinical Psychology Review* 2: 409–20.

Callahan, J. 1989. How many survivors of suicide are there? Part two. *Surviving Suicide* (a newsletter of the American Association of Suicidology) 1 no. 2: 1, 4.

Carlson, T. 1995. *The suicide of my son: A story of childhood depression.* Duluth, MN: Benline Press.

Chance, S. 1988. Surviving suicide: A journey to resolution. *Bulletin of the Menninger Clinic* 52: 30–39.

Chance, S. 1992. *Stronger than death: When suicide touches your life.* New York: Norton.

Clarke, J. 1989. *Life after grief: A soul journey after suicide.* Marietta, GA: Personal Pathways Press.

Cleiren, M. P. H. D., R. F. W. Diekstra, A. J. F. M. Kerkhof, and J. van der Wal. 1994. Mode of death and kinship in bereavement: Focusing on "who" rather than "how." *Crisis* 15: 22–36.

Cleiren, M. P. H. D., O. Grad, A. Zavasnik, and R. F. W. Diekstra. 1996. Psychosocial impact of bereavement after suicide and fatal traffic accident: A comparative two-country study. *Acta Psychiatrica Scandinavica* 94: 37–44.

Constantino, R. E., and P. L. Bricker 1996. Nursing postvention for spousal survivors of suicide. *Issues in Mental Health Nursing* 17: 131–52.

Cullen, J. 1988. Joan Rivers shares her grief. *Ladies' Home Journal*, April, 46, 48, 50, 148, 150.

Dalke, D. 1994. Therapy-assisted growth after parental suicide: From a personal and professional perspective. *Omega* 29: 113–51.

Dunne, E. J. 1987. Surviving the suicide of a therapist. In *Suicide and its aftermath: Understanding and counseling the survivors,* edited by E. J. Dunne, J. L. McIntosh and K. L. Dunne-Maxim. 142–48. New York: Norton.

Dunne, E., and M. M. Wilbur. 1993. *Survivors of suicide* [pamphlet]. Washington, DC: American Association of Suicidology.

Farberow, N. L. 1992. The Los Angeles Survivors-after-Suicide program: An evaluation. *Crisis* 13: 23–34.

Fine, C. 1996. *No time to say goodbye: Surviving the suicide of a loved one.* New York: Doubleday.

Foster, B. 1987. Suicide and the impact on the therapist. In *Attachment and the therapeutic process: Essays in honor of Otto Allen Will, Jr., M.D.,* edited by J. L. Sacksteder, D. P. Schwartz, and Y. Akabane. 197–204. Madison, CT: International Universities Press.

Gorkin, M. 1985. On the suicide of one's patient. *Bulletin of the Menninger Clinic* 49: 1–9.

Grad, O. T., and A. Zavasnik. 1996. Similarities and differences in the process of bereavement after suicide and after traffic fatalities in Slovenia. *Omega* 33: 243–51.

Graves, J. S. 1978. Adolescents and their psychiatrist's suicide: A study of shared grief and mourning. *Journal of the American Academy of Child Psychiatry* 17: 521–32.

Grossman, J. A., D. A. Clark, D. Gross, L. Halstead, and J. Pennington. 1995. Child bereavement after paternal suicide. *Journal of Child and Adolescent Psychiatric Nursing* 8: 5–17.

Harness-Overly, P. 1992. *A message of hope: For surviving the tragedy of suicide.* Upland, CA: Bradley Press.

Hartley, M., and A. Commire. (1990). *Breaking the silence.* New York: Signet Books.

Hebert, D. 1987. My brother Tim and me. In *Suicide and its aftermath: Understanding and counseling the survivors*, edited by E. J. Dunne, J. L. McIntosh and K. L. Dunne-Maxim. 95–103. New York: Norton.

Heilig, S. M. 1983. Reaction of a therapist to the suicide of a patient. In *Proceedings, sixteenth annual meeting of the American Association of Suicidology*, edited by C. Vorkoper and K. Smith. 73–74. Denver, CO: American Association of Suicidology.

Henslin, J. M. 1971. Problems and prospects in studying significant others of suicides. *Bulletin of Suicidology*. no. 8, 81–84.

Hoffman, Y. 1987. Surviving a child's suicide. *American Journal of Nursing* 87: 955–56.

Hopmeyer, E., and A. Werk. 1994. A comparative study of family bereavement groups. *Death Studies* 18: 243–56.

Horowitz, M. J., and R. Hammer. 1976. The suicide of a friend. In *Stress response syndromes*, by M. J. Horowitz. 337–51. New York: Jason Aronson.

Hurley, D. J. 1991. The crisis of paternal suicide: Case of Cathy, age 4 1/2. In *Play therapy with children in crisis: A casebook for practitioners*, edited by N. B. Webb. 237–53. New York: Guilford.

Ilan, E. 1973. The impact of a father's suicide on his latency son. In *The child in his family: The impact of disease and death, Vol. 2*, edited by E. J. Anthony and C. Koupernik. 299–306. New York: Wiley.

Interaction: Survivors of suicide. 1996. *Newslink* (quarterly publication of the American Association of Suicidology) 22 no: 3. 3, 15.

Jakab, I., and M. C. Howard, 1969. Art therapy with a 12-year-old girl who witnessed suicide and developed school phobia. *Psychotherapy and Psychosomatics* 17: 309–24.

Jones, F. A., Jr. 1987. Therapists as survivors of client suicide. In *Suicide and its aftermath: Understanding and counseling the survivors*, edited by E. J. Dunne, J. L. McIntosh and K. L. Dunne-Maxim. 126–41. New York: Norton.

Krementz, J. 1981. Jack Hopkins, age 8, 9–15, Thomas Joseph, age 14, 85–87. In *How it feels when a parent dies*. New York: Knopf.

Langford, M. 1989. *That nothing be wasted: My experience with the suicide of my son*. New Hope, AL: Woman's Missionary Union.

Lockridge, L. 1995. Least likely suicide: The search for my father, Ross

Lockridge, Jr., author of *Raintree County*. *Suicide and Life-Threatening Behavior* 25: 489–98.

McIntosh, J. L. 1985–86. Survivors of suicide: A comprehensive bibliography. *Omega* 16: 355–70.

McIntosh, J. L. 1987a. Research, therapy, and educational needs. In *Suicide and its aftermath: Understanding and counseling the survivors*, edited by E. J. Dunne, J. L. McIntosh and K. L. Dunne-Maxim. 263–77. New York: Norton.

McIntosh, J. L. 1987b. Survivor family relationships: Literature review. In *Suicide and its aftermath: Understanding and counseling the survivors*, edited by E. J. Dunne, J. L. McIntosh and K. L. Dunne-Maxim. 73–84. New York: Norton.

McIntosh, J. L. 1989. How many survivors of suicide are there? *Surviving Suicide* (a newsletter of the American Association of Suicidology). 1 no. 1: 1, 4.

McIntosh, J. L. 1993. Control group studies of suicide survivors: A review and critique. *Suicide and Life-Threatening Behavior* 23: 146–61.

McIntosh, J. L. 1996. Survivors of suicide: A comprehensive bibliography update, 1986–1995. *Omega* 33:147–75

McIntosh, J. L. June 24 1997. *U.S.A. suicide: 1995 official final data* [suicide data page]. Washington, DC: American Association of Suicidology.

Moon, S. 1986. I shall not perish: A survivor speaks. *Thanatos*, Spring, 2–5.

Murphy, S. A. 1996. Parent bereavement stress and preventive intervention following the violent deaths of adolescent or young adult children. *Death Studies* 20: 441–52.

Murphy, S. A., R. Baugher, J. Lohan, J. Scheideman, J. Heerwagen, L. C. Johnson, L. Tillery, and M. C. Grover. 1996. Parents' evaluation of a preventive intervention following the sudden, violent deaths of their children. *Death Studies* 20: 453–68.

Nelson, B. J., and T. T. Frantz. 1996. Family interactions of suicide survivors and survivors of non-suicidal death. *Omega* 33: 131–46.

Organ, T. 1979. Grief and the art of consolation: A personal testimony. *The Christian Century* 96: 759–62.

Pesaresi, J. 1987. When one of us is gone. In *Suicide and its aftermath: Understanding and counseling the survivors*, edited by E. J. Dunne, J. L. McIntosh and K. L. Dunne-Maxim. 104–108. New York: Norton.

Pfeffer, C. R., P. Martins, J. Mann, M. Sunkenberg, A. Ice, J. P. Damore, Jr., C. Gallo, I. Karpenos, and H. Jiang. 1997. Child survivors of suicide: Psychosocial characteristics. *Journal of the American Academy of Child and Adolescent Psychiatry* 36: 65–74.

Reed, M. D. 1993. Sudden death and bereavement outcomes: The impact of resources on grief symptomatology and detachment. *Suicide and Life-Threatening Behavior* 23: 204–20.

Rivers, J., with R. Meryman. 1991. *Still talking*. New York: Turtle Bay Books.

Rivers, J., with R. Schoenstein. 1997. *Bouncing back: How to survive anything. & I mean anything*. New York: HarperCollins.

Rogers, J., A. Sheldon, C. Barwick, K. Letofsky, and W. Lancee. 1982. Help for families of suicide: Survivors support group. *Canadian Journal of Psychiatry* 27: 444–49.

Ross, E. B. 1990. *After suicide: A ray of hope*. Iowa City, IA: Lynn Publications.

Ross, E. B. 1997. *Life after suicide: A ray of hope for those left behind*. New York: Plenum.

Rubey, C. T. 1985. LOSS. In *Proceedings eighteenth annual meeting American Association of Suicidology*, edited by R. Cohen-Sandler. 114–16. Denver, CO: American Association of Suicidology.

Rubey, C. T., and J. L. McIntosh. 1996. Suicide survivors groups: Results of a survey. *Suicide and Life-Threatening Behavior* 26: 351–58.

Rudestam, K. E. 1987. Public perception of suicide survivors. In *Suicide and its aftermath: Understanding and counseling the survivors*, edited by E. J. Dunne, J. L. McIntosh, and K. L. Dunne-Maxim. 31–44. New York: Norton.

Rudestam, K. E. 1990. Survivors of suicide: Research and speculations. In *Current concepts of suicide*, edited by D. Lester. 203–13. Philadelphia: Charles Press.

Séguin, M., A. Lesage, and M. C. Kiely. 1995. Parental bereavement after suicide and accident: A comparative study. *Suicide and Life-Threatening Behavior* 25: 489–98.

Shneidman, E. S. 1969. Prologue: Fifty-eight years. In *On the nature of suicide*, edited by E. S. Shneidman. 1–30. San Francisco: Jossey-Bass.

Silverman, E., L. Range, and J. Overholser. 1994–95. Bereavement from suicide as compared to other forms of bereavement. *Omega* 30: 41–51.

Silverman, P. R. 1972. Intervention with the widow of a suicide. In *Survivors of suicide*, edited by A. C. Cain. 186–214. Springfield, IL: Thomas.

Thompson, K. E., and L. M. Range. 1992–93. Bereavement following suicide and other deaths: Why support attempts fail. *Omega* 26: 61–70.

Van Dongen, C. J. 1993. Social context of postsuicide bereavement. *Death Studies* 17: 125–41.

White-Bowden, S. 1985. *Everything to live for: A mother's story of her teenage son's suicide.* New York: Poseidon Press.

Wrobleski, A. 1984–85. The Suicide survivors grief group. *Omega* 15: 173–84.

Wrobleski, A. 1994. *Suicide: Survivors—A guide for those left behind* 2d ed. Minneapolis: Afterwords.

Selected Annotated Bibliography

This selected bibliography is intended as an overview of resources available for survivors of suicide. Survivors will also be interested in the references and the table in the preceding essay by John L. McIntosh.

Alexander, V. 1991. *Words I never thought to speak: Stories of life in the wake of suicide*. New York: Lexington Books. Although neither its focus nor a highlighted aspect of the work, Ms. Alexander's book includes reflections by five adult children survivors, including the author and a brother and sister. See below.

Bolton, I., with C. Mitchell. 1983. *My son, my son.: A guide to healing after a suicide in the family*. Atlanta: Bolton Press. The groundbreaking work by a survivor of suicide. For good reason, it is often the first book placed in the hands of a survivor.

Cain, A. C., ed. 1972. *Survivors of suicide*. Springfield, IL: Charles C. Thomas.

Colt, G. H. 1991. *The Enigma of Suicide*. New York: Summit Books. This impressive work contains a lengthy section on the general characteristics of grief following a suicide.

Dunne, E. J., J. L. McIntosh and K. L. Dunne-Maxim, eds. 1987. *Suicide and its aftermath: Understanding and counseling the survivors.* New York: W.W. Norton & Company. The section on "The Aftermath of Suicide in Families" presents an account by a daughter (V. Alexander, see below) who was an adult when her mother died.

Dunne, E., and M. M. Wilbur. 1993. *Survivors of suicide* [pamphlet]. Washington, DC: American Association of Suicidology.

Grollman, E. A. 1971. *Suicide: Prevention, intervention, postvention*. Boston: Beacon Press.

Hewett, J. H. 1980. *After Suicide*. Philadelphia: The Westminster Press.

Lukas, C., and H. M. Seiden. 1987. *Silent grief: Living in the wake of suicide*. New York: Bantam Books. A first-class treatment of grief after suicide.

One unusual feature of this book is that it addresses, albeit briefly, the effect on sexuality of surviving a suicide. This area is rarely mentioned in the literature, yet it is a significant one for adult children survivors.

Ross, E. B. 1990. *After suicide: A ray of hope*. Iowa City, IA: Lynn Publications. A comprehensive description of the experience of surviving a suicide and an invitation to transform the loss into growth. Already a classic for survivors.

Ross, E. B. 1997. *Life after suicide: A ray of hope for those left behind*. New York: Plenum. A revised and updated edition of *After Suicide*. Features an extensive and updated bibliography.

Schneider, J. M. 1994. *Finding my way: Healing and transformation through loss and grief*. Colfax, WI: Seasons Press. Although not directly related to suicide, this book, written by a psychologist, offers a model of grief that is holistic and ultimately life-affirming.

Wertheimer, A. 1991. A *Special Scar: The experiences of people bereaved by suicide*. London: Routledge. Written for British survivors, this is an outstanding survey of the grief occasioned by suicide. Based on fifty survivor interviews, Wertheimer ably describes and comments upon a broad range of survivor experiences.

Wrobleski, A. 1994. *Suicide: Survivors—A guide for those left behind* (2d ed.). Minneapolis: Afterwords. A compassionate and thorough portrait of grief following suicide. Along with Bolton and Ross, one of the standards of this genre.

Texts by adult children survivors of suicide

Alexander, V. 1987. Living through my mother's suicide. In *Suicide and its aftermath: Understanding and counseling the survivors*, edited by E. J. Dunne, J. L. McIntosh and K. L. Dunne-Maxim. 109–17. New York: Norton.

Alexander, V. 1991. Author's Story, "Natalie," and "Susan and Philip." In *Words I never thought to speak: Stories of life in the wake of suicide*. New York: Lexington Books.

Hartley, M., and A. Commire. 1990. *Breaking the silence*. New York: Signet Books.

Directory of Suicide Survivor Support Groups

All varieties of survivor of suicide support groups are available nationwide. The following list is a representative sample of such groups. Many other groups exist. Contact the American Association of Suicidology, the listed organizations, and local hospitals for information about the support resources in your area. When inquiring about a support group, consider such questions as: What is the leadership structure (peer or professional)? How often does the group meet? Is there a fee? The American Association of Suicidology maintains listings for support groups worldwide:

American Association of
  Suicidology
Suite 310, 4201 Connecticut
  Avenue, NW
Washington, DC 20008
(202) 237-2282

Some of the telephone numbers
  listed are to private homes.

Alabama

Crisis Center, Inc.
3600 8th Avenue S., Suite 501
Birmingham, AL 35222
(205) 323-7782

Alaska

Support Group for Suicide
  Survivors
Alaska Police Chaplains'
  Ministries

Chaplains Office
P.O. Box 200654
Anchorage, AK 99520-0654
(907) 272-3100

Fairbanks Crisis Line
P.O. Box 70908
Fairbanks, AK 99707
(907) 451-8600 or (800) 898-5463

Arizona

Survivors of Suicide
Help on Call Crisis Line
P.O. Box 43696
Tuscon, AZ 85733
(602) 323-9373

Arkansas

Survivors of Suicide
3925 Renee Drive
Jonesboro, AR 72404-8577

S.O.S. Arkansas Chapter
Rt. 7, Box 138
Malvern, AR 72104
(501) 337-1930 or (501) 686-6957

California

The Institute for Suicide
    Prevention, Inc.
3130 Wilshire Blvd., Suite 550
Los Angeles, CA 90403
(213) 386-2622

Self Help Grief Group
Center for Elderly Suicide
Prevention and Grief
3626 Geary Boulevard
San Francisco, CA 94118
(415) 750-5355

Sharing & Healing
3586 Trenton Avenue
San Diego, CA 92117
(619) 272-3760 or (619) 272-1759

Colorado

Heartbeat
710 33rd Street
Boulder, CO 80303
(303) 444-3496

Heartbeat
2956 South Wolff
Denver, CO 80236
(303) 934-8464

Connecticut

Safe Place
The Samaritans of the Capital
    Region
P.O. Box 12004
Hartford, CT 06112
(203) 232-2121

Survivors of Suicide
68 Hillbrook Road
Wilton, CT 08697
(203) 762-7804

Delaware

S.O.S.
Grace United Methodist Church
Church and Morris Streets
Millsboro, DE 19966
(302) 537-9520

S.O.S.
1813 N. Franklin Street
Wilmington, DE 19802
(302) 656-8308

Florida

Self Help Support Group
Suicide Prevention Center
2134 Bo Peep Drive West
Jacksonville, FL 32210-2918
(904) 353-2223

Connections
13302-B Winding Oak Court
Tampa, FL 33612-3416
(813) 932-1722

Georgia

S.O.S. Sandy Springs Chapter
The Link Counseling Center
348 Mt. Vernon Highway, NE
Atlanta, GA 30328
(404) 256-9797

Roswell Group
Roswell United Methodist Church
814 Mimosa Boulevard
Roswell, GA 30075
(770) 993-6218 ext. 116

Hawaii

Survivors of Suicide
Helping Hands of Hawaii
680 Iwilei Road, #430
Honolulu, HI 96817
(808) 521-4555

Idaho

Survivors of Suicide
4917 West Catalpa
Boise, ID 83703
(208) 338-1017 (Leader's home)

Survivors of Suicide, Inc.
2411 South Woodruff
Idaho Falls, ID 83404
(208) 522-0033 or (208) 524-2411

Illinois

Loving Outreach to Survivors of
    Suicide
Catholic Charities
126 North Desplaines Street
Chicago, IL 60661-2357
(312) 655-7283

Suicide: Survivors Gather
Fred C. Olson Funeral Chapels
309 7th Street
Rockford, IL 61104
(815) 962-0782

Indiana

SOS/Heartbeat
2341 Winding Brook Circle
Bloomington, IN 47401-4373
(812) 334-3801

Survivors of Suicide Victims
Chaplains' Office
Community Hospital of Indianapolis
Indianapolis, IN 46219
(317) 841-5269

Iowa

Suicide Survivors Group
Foundation II, Inc.
1540 Second Avenue SE
Cedar Rapids, IA 52403
(319) 362-2174 or (800) 332-4224

Ray of Hope, Inc.
P.O. Box 2323
Iowa City, IA 52244
(319) 337-9890

Kansas

Suicide Prevention Program
Parsons Ray of Hope
203 Kay Lane
Parsons, KS 67357
(316) 421-3254

Survivors of Suicide
3019 S.E. Starlite
Topeka, KS 66605
(913) 267-4547

Kentucky

Survivors of Suicide
Hospice of the Bluegrass
2312 Alexandria Drive
Lexington, KY 40504
(606) 276-5344

Survivors of Suicide Inc.
330 North Hubbard's Lane
Louisville, KY 40207
(502) 895-9122

Louisiana

Support After Suicide
3904 Gouville Drive
Monroe, LA 71202
(318) 323-9479

Coping with Suicide
406 Audubon Trace
New Orleans, LA 70121-1553
(504) 865-2670

Maine

Safe Place
All Souls Church
State Street
Bangor, ME 04401
(207) 947-7003

Suicide Survivors Group
Maine Medical Center
22 Bramhill Street
Portland, ME 04102
(207) 871-4226

Maryland

Seasons: Suicide Bereavement
4706 Meise Drive
Baltimore, MD 21206
(410) 882-2937

Seasons: Suicide Bereavement
13907 Vista Drive
Rockville, MD 20853
(301) 460-4677

Massachusetts

After Suicide
41 Concord Square
Boston, MA 02118
(617) 738-7668

Safe Place/Samaritans
Samaritans, Suburban West
276 Union Avenue
Framingham, MA 01702
(508) 875-4500 or (508) 478-7877

Michigan

Survivors of Suicide
NSO Emergency Telephone
    Service/
SP Center
220 Bagley, Suite 626
Detroit, MI 48226
(313) 224-7000

SOS Group
Health Source Hospital
3340 Hospital Road
Saginaw, MI 48603
(517) 781-0410

Minnesota

Suicide Survivors Support Group
St. Mary's Grief Support Center
407 East Third Street
Duluth, MN 55805
(218) 726-4402

Death Response Team
University of Minnesota
Comstock Hall East Housing Service
210 Delaware Street, SE
Minneapolis, MN 55455-0307
(612) 624-4632

Mississippi

Survivors of Suicide
First Baptist Church
P.O. Box 250
Jackson, MS 39205-0250
(601) 825-7888

Missouri

Survivors of Suicide Support Group
#8 Terrapin Road
Cape Giradeau, MO 63701
(573) 334-6508

Survivors of Suicide Support
   Group
Life Crisis Services, Inc.
1423 South Big Bend Boulevard
St. Louis, MO 63117
(314) 647-3100

Montana

Surviving Friends, Inc.
402 Crestline Drive
Missoula, MT 59803
(406) 543-6132

Nebraska

Lincoln Ray of Hope
2118 South 36th Street
Lincoln, NE 68506
(402) 488-3827

S.O.S. Omaha
6114 Franklin Street
Omaha, NE 68104
(402) 558-4616

Nevada

Suicide Prevention & Crisis Call
   Center
P.O. Box 8016
Reno, NV 89507
(702) 784-8085

New Hampshire

S.O.S. Survivors of Suicide
Samaritans of South Central NH
2013 Elm Street
Manchester, NH 03104
(603) 644-2525 or (603) 622-3836

New Jersey

Survivors of Suicide
P.O. Box 183
Andover, NJ 07821-0183
(201) 786-5178

Survivors of Suicide
UMDNJ University Behavioral
   Health Care
671 Hoes Lane
Piscataway, NJ 08854
(908) 235-4109

New Mexico

Survivors of Suicide
12010 Dusty Rose Road, NE
Albuquerque, NM 87122
(505) 858-1240

Survivors of Suicide
2210 Miguel Chavez Road,
   #1812
Santa Fe, NM 87505
(505) 984-8203 or (505) 473-2885

New York

Safe Place
The Samaritans
P.O. Box 5228
Albany, NY 12205
(518) 459-4040

The Samaritans of New York
P.O. Box 1259
Madison Square Station
New York, NY 10159
(212) 673-3000

After Suicide
34 Alford Street
Rochester, NY 14609
(716) 654-7262

North Carolina

Touched by Suicide
To Life
1850 East 5th Street, Suite 212
Charlotte, NC 28204
(704) 332-5433

Triangle Hospice
Lifeline Suicide Survivor Support
1804 Martin Luther King, Jr. Parkway
  Suite 112
Durham, NC 27707
(919) 490-8480

North Dakota

Grief After Suicide
MH Association of North Dakota
200 West Bowen Avenue
Bismarck, ND 58504
(701) 255-3692 or (800) 472-2911

Suicide Survivor Support Group
P.O. Box 447
Fargo, ND 58107
(701) 293-6462

Ohio

Cincinnati Survivors After Suicide
4142 Eddystone Drive
Cincinnati, OH 45251
(513) 385-6110

Survivors of Suicide
192 South Princeton Avenue
Columbus, OH 43223
(614) 279-9382

Oklahoma

Survivors of Suicide
4400 West Main, #120
Norman, OK 73072
(405) 447-1498 or (405) 366-7807

Survivors
Mental Health Association
1870 South Boulder
Tulsa, OK 74119
(918) 585-1213 or (918) 663-0747

Oregon

Suicide Bereavement
  Support
P.O. Box 12471
Portland, OR 97212
(503) 235-0476

Pennsylvania

Survivors of Suicide, Inc.
The Graduate Hospital
18th and Lombard Streets
Philadelphia, PA 19146
(215) 545-2242

Survivors of Suicide
Western Psychiatric Institute
  and Clinic
3811 O'Hara Street
Pittsburgh, PA 15213
(412) 624-5170

Rhode Island

Safe Place/Samaritans
2 Magee Street
Providence, RI 02906
(401) 272-4044 or (800) 365-4044

South Carolina

Survivors of Suicide
Mental Health Association of
  Greenville County
301 University Ridge, Suite 3600
Greenville, SC 29601
(864) 271-8888

Survivors of Suicide
P.O. Box 71583
North Charleston, SC 29415-1583
(803) 747-3007 or (803) 744-4357

South Dakota

SOS Group
Heartbeat
P.O. Box 646
Huron, SD 57350
(605) 352-6263 or (605) 352-7152

Survivors of Suicide
Family Services
3700 South Kiwanis Avenue, Suite 4
Sioux Falls, SD 57105
(605) 336-1974

Tennessee

Survivors of Suicide Support Groups
Crisis Intervention Center, Inc.
P.O. Box 40752
Nashville, TN 37204-0752
(615) 244-7444 or (615) 269-4357

Texas

Suicide and Crisis Center
2808 Swiss Avenue
Dallas, TX 75204
(214) 828-1000

Crisis Intervention of Houston, Inc.
P.O. Box 130866
Houston, TX 77219-0866
(713) 527-9864 or (713) 228-1505

Utah

Legacy
2684 North 2700 East
Layton, UT 84040
(801) 771-8476 or (801) 394-5556

Seasons
P.O. Box 187
Park City, UT 84060
(801) 649-8327

Virginia

Suicide Survivor Support Group
3601 Devilwood Court
Fairfax, VA 22030
(703) 866-2100 or (703) 273-3454

Surviving Group
Richmond Behavioral Health
    Authority
Crisis Intervention and Intake
    Services
501 North 9th Street, #205
Richmond, VA 23219-1544
(804) 780-6911

Washington

Survivors of Suicide
Crisis Clinic of King County
1515 Dexter Avenue North, Suite
    300
Seattle, WA 98109
(206) 461-3210 or (206) 461-3222

Thurston County Survivors
    Group
Lifeline Institute for Suicide
    Prevention
9108 Lakewood Drive, SW
Tacoma, WA 98499
(360) 438-6887 or (360) 422-2552

West Virginia

Survivors of Suicide
107 Lee Street
Ripley, WV 25271
(304) 372-4290 or (304) 372-3493

Suicide Survivors Support
  Group
P.O. Box 4043
Warwood Post Office
Wheeling, WV 26003
(304) 277-3916

Wisconsin

Survivors of Suicide
625 West Washington Avenue
Madison, WI 53703
(608) 251-2345

Survivors Helping Survivors
Mental Health Association in
  Milwaukee City
734 North Fourth Street, Suite 325
Milwaukee, WI 53203-2102
(414) 276-3122

Wyoming

Share and Care Group
1108 West 27th Street
Cheyenne, WY 82001
(307) 637-3753 or (307) 638-8642

Index